Votewise Now!

Votewise Now!

Helping Christians engage with the issues

Edited by
Rose Lynas

First published in Great Britain in 2009

Society for Promoting Christian Knowledge
36 Causton Street
London SW1P 4ST

British Library Cataloguing-in-Publication Data
A catalogue record for this book is available from the British Library

ISBN 978–0–281–06192–1

10 9 8 7 6 5 4 3 2 1

Designed and typeset by Kenneth Burnley, Wirral, Cheshire
Printed in Great Britain by CPI Bookmarque, Croydon

Produced on paper from sustainable forests

Contents

About the Jubilee Centre   vii

Foreword by Joel Edwards   ix

Acknowledgements   xi

Introduction: Why *Votewise*?   1

1   The Economy   PAUL WILLIAMS   15

2   Criminal Justice   JONATHAN BURNSIDE   24

3   Health Care   ANDREW FERGUSSON   33

4   Education   TREVOR COOLING   41

5   The Environment   HILARY MARLOW   50

6   International Order   BENEDICT ROGERS   60

7   Nationhood and Immigration   DEWI HUGHES with ROSE LYNAS   68

8   Tax and Benefits   JO HOLLAND   77

9   Employment   MARTIN CLARK   86

10   Housing   PETER LYNAS   94

11   Time for the Conservatives?   ALISTAIR BURT MP   105

12   Why Vote Liberal Democrat?   TIM FARRON MP   108

13   Why Vote Labour?   SHARON HODGSON MP   111

Conclusion: How Do I Respond?   114

About the Jubilee Centre

The Jubilee Centre explores a wide range of social, economic and political issues, seeking to provide a positive response to the challenges faced by individuals, communities and policy-makers in the twenty-first century from a distinctively faith-based perspective.

Our vision is for a movement of organizations, churches and individual Christians to advance a coherent and positively-stated biblical social agenda that is of benefit to the whole of society. We believe that the Bible presents a coherent social vision, based on right relationships, that provides an alternative to contemporary political ideologies. The Jubilee Centre has applied this relational agenda to areas as diverse as the economy, criminal justice, care for the elderly, asylum and immigration, the environment, and sexual ethics.

Our publications include *Just Sex: Is It Ever Just Sex?* by Guy Brandon, which launched the Fair Sex Movement, the groundbreaking *Jubilee Manifesto*, and the quarterly 'Cambridge Papers' – an influential collection of peer-reviewed studies. We also maintain an extensive blog and offer a wide range of reports, videos and class/small-group discussion materials on our website, most of which can be freely downloaded.

For regularly updated comment on all the issues as we approach – and move beyond – the election, visit the Jubilee Centre blog, at <www.jubilee-centre.org>.

To find out more, please contact us at: Jubilee Centre, 3 Hooper Street, Cambridge CB1 2NZ.

Tel: 01223 566319
Email: <info@jubilee-centre.org>
Website: <www.jubilee-centre.org>

Foreword

The Revd Dr Joel Edwards is the International Director for Micah Challenge. Prior to this, Joel was General Director of the Evangelical Alliance UK. He also serves as a Commissioner on the Equality and Human Rights Commission for the UK and as an Advisory Member of Tony Blair's Faith Foundation.

When the previous edition of *Votewise* landed on my desk I welcomed it with open arms. As the then General Director of the Evangelical Alliance and someone who was likely to be asked to comment on our response to a general election, I found it an invaluable tool not only as a Christian leader but, even more importantly, as a voting citizen.

Everyone who is eligible to do so should vote; but it's another thing to vote wisely. *Votewise Now!* leaves us with no excuse. This book is an agenda for Christians, not just in response to the electoral process but as an ongoing tool for responsible citizenship – and for a number of reasons. First, it pools the wisdom of informed Christians to guide us through a number of key issues on which elections are fought and lost such as the economy, health and education. But it does more than that: it also helps us to go beyond our domestic preoccupations to the wider issues facing our global village by highlighting some issues such as international order and the environment.

I also appreciated the commitment to the value of party politics. As we prepare for the ballot box we need to take seriously the fact that Britain is a leading democracy – not a theocracy. Political choice is an integral part of our democracy, and I love the fact that in this book diversity is celebrated. We really should not underestimate the value of having Christian MPs who respect each other and speak with passion and conviction about their own political allegiance.

You don't need to be a political scientist to know that British politics and relationships stand at an important crossroads. How we vote and how we govern in the years ahead will be about much more than British politics. We are a key member of the global political village, and what we do over the next decade will have global repercussions. And that political village is shifting its composition and global chemistry with amazing frequency across Europe and America.

Leaders cannot lead without a mandate, and the inexorable democratization of our nations which is spreading through business and the ballot is changing the political landscape, from America to Iraq. When we enter the privacy of the ballot what we do there contributes to the cacophony of voices and the decisions which will shape the future of our village.

No one votes alone, and no vote is an island activity. This means we need all the wise votes we can get.

Joel Edwards

Acknowledgements

Votewise Now! follows on from, and therefore owes much to, its first edition, *Votewise*, written by Nick Spencer. Nick's work provided the necessary springboard, and framework, for the current edition.

The chapter editors contributed the majority of the ideas, challenges and inspiration. Their wise words made the editing process an enjoyable and easy one.

John Hayward, Guy Brandon and Alan White from the Jubilee Centre provided invaluable support. From Relationships Foundation: Martin Eden facilitated the political contacts and generously offered prudent counsel along the way; Michael Trend read key sections and gave sage literary and political advice.

Particular thanks go to the Bible Society, Evangelical Alliance and one key individual, without whose financial support this new edition and accompanying resources would not have been possible.

A special thank you must go to Peter Lynas who gave tirelessly, patiently and willingly to this project. His contributions cannot be overestimated.

This book would not exist without the input of those named, as well as the many unnamed sources of inspiration that we all inevitably draw from. The end result is, I hope, a rich and thought-provoking text. Any remaining mistakes are mine alone.

Lastly, I would like to thank the Jubilee Centre for inviting me to be part of this exciting and important project.

Rose Lynas
Cambridge

Introduction: Why *Votewise?*

Faith and politics

The coat-hangers in the Members' cloakroom in Parliament all have a red ribbon attached to them so that MPs may safely store their swords before entering the chamber. As Lord Carey commented, 'In the modern world there is great pressure to treat faith in the same way – to put it safely aside before entering our workplaces, and to pick it up again at the end of the day.'[1]

When former Labour Prime Minister Tony Blair was asked about his Christian faith, Alastair Campbell silenced his reply saying, 'I'm sorry, we don't do God.' Only after stepping down as Prime Minister did Blair admit the importance of his faith and explain why he never discussed it: 'If you are in the American political system or others, then you can talk about religious faith and people say "Yes, that's fair enough" and it is something they respond to quite naturally. You talk about it in our system and, frankly, people think you're a nutter.'[2]

Politics is the process by which groups of people make decisions – decisions that affect significant areas of our lives. *Votewise Now!*, as the title suggests, has been written to stimulate wise thinking about, and involvement in, important current political issues. Alistair Campbell's suggestion that private faith has no place in politics is wrong; there is no such thing as neutral, value-free or even moral-free ground. In voting, Christians must make, and act upon, the important connections between what we believe and how we live. The Bible rejects the sacred–secular, public–private divide. We are whole people created to live whole and holy lives.

Kingdom values

Some Christians have neglected the earthly responsibilities of their heavenly (kingdom) citizenship, believing such matters as politics to be outside their, or even the Bible's, concern. However, even a scant reading of the biblical text reveals its political nature, embodied by its central characters. We read of kings and rulers, of Esther the lobbyist approaching the king on behalf of her people, and Daniel the senior civil servant or cabinet minister speaking truth in a foreign land. Jesus incarnated a message which threatened the political authorities and led to his execution. The kingdom of God is a political statement. Christ is Messiah and Lord, not Caesar or any other political ruler. The Bible is replete with calls to seek justice, fight the cause of the widow and orphan, and stand against the oppressor – all part of 'loving God and loving our neighbour'. Indeed, it could be argued that Christians in particular have a political mandate requiring them to be involved, seeking ways that God's will 'may be done on earth as it is in heaven', that his kingdom will come, overthrowing false and misused claims to authority and power.

Christians are called to be a chosen people, a royal priesthood, a holy nation, a people belonging to God (1 Peter 2.9). We are to be a light to the nations around us, concerned with love, justice and righteousness. The biblical vision for creation is for right relationships. The biblical narrative begins with a man and woman relating rightly with their creator, one another and the rest of creation. The human rebellion of Genesis 3 has a profound and ongoing effect on each of these relationships, causing fear, shame, blame, suffering and abuse. Reconciliation and redemption are the motifs of the biblical story as the creator reaches out, yearning to be in fellowship with his creation. The story climaxes in the incarnation of Jesus Christ the God–man, and is fulfilled as he cries out from the cross, 'It is finished.' *Shalom* – completeness, wholeness and restored relationships – is initiated in earthly history. God's kingdom breaks in turning the world upside down or, more accurately, right side up. So we live in the time of the 'now and the not yet', giving equal weight to the two comings of Jesus – what he has done and what he will do. The kingdom is now inaugurated, but not yet consummated.

God is in the business of putting right the whole cosmos (Colossians 1), bringing order out of chaos, resolving conflict and restoring relationships, working for justice and just solutions in all situations. Everything we do to counter, resist or oppose the effects of Genesis 3 is a participation in God's redeeming and transforming work, and looks forward to the completion of this work. We work as agents and signs of God's redeeming work. Our role as Christians is to engage in acts of stewardship, service, creativity, innovation, witness, truth-telling, preservation, healing, community building, justice and peacemaking.

Why vote?

Seventy-one per cent of the British electorate cast their vote in 1997, but this dropped to 59 per cent in 2001, rising slightly to 61 per cent at the last general election. Among 18–24-year-olds it is estimated that only 37 per cent voted in 2005.[3] Apathy is a problem – though one positive consequence is that as fewer people vote, the votes of those who do show up count for more.

In the United States, voter turnout dropped below 50 per cent in 1996, but almost 62 per cent of the voting population participated in the election of Barack Obama. A strong candidate and a close election may encourage more voters in the UK. The next general election is likely to be close, and many commentators suggest that a hung Parliament is a distinct possibility, though British voters have a history of swinging decisively between parties. Polling in the UK shows that after a strong start as Prime Minister, Gordon Brown and the Labour Party are suffering. That said, throughout 2008 and into 2009, the party consistently polled in the mid-thirties. Over the same period, support for the Conservatives strengthened under David Cameron, levelling out around the 40 per cent mark, while the Liberal Democrats struggled below the 20 per cent mark.

It is worth noting that in 2005 Labour won 355 seats (out of 646) with 35.3 per cent of the vote. The Conservatives won 32.3 per cent of the vote but only won 198 seats, and the Liberal Democrats only won 62 seats despite receiving 22.1 per cent of the vote. The parties are acutely aware that while voter share is important, it is seats won that counts. The Liberal Democrats' support for proportional representation is not surprising, as they would have won over 140 seats under the system, based on their 2005 election share.

Trust

Apathy and declining voter turnout have been linked to a decline in trust in politicians. The 'expenses scandal' exposed MPs' abuse of the public's trust and money, exploiting the rules instead of questioning their premise. These issues are no private matter: if politicians can be untruthful or misleading about their expenses, why not about other issues? However, it is a sad reflection on society that an MP is pressured to stand down over a duck house, but not for 'entertaining' a prostitute in his office. Voters must hold their politicians to account for all their actions, and not just fixate on the 'bottom line'.

It is important to remember that the British government, for all its problems, is one of the least corrupt political systems in the world. Voters must retain perspective, channelling their passionate energy into positive action. Indeed, such problems as we have recently witnessed should, if anything, provoke wiser voter engagement with the political system, inspiring the creation of a transparent system that renews trust. It is the role of the citizen to hold the politicians to account. We cannot pass judgement and not be involved in a solution. It is those who turn up who make the difference, and no citizen is absolved from this responsibility. While it is very difficult for an MP to be dismissed, it is within the voters' power not to return them.

Voting as an act of worship

Voting, then, is not simply a right or a responsibility but is part of our worship, an act of loving service to God and our neighbour. Voting integrates the theological and the political. As we make our mark at the ballot box we bring together religious faith and social values. Faith and politics belong together. Our task as Christians is not simply to study God's word for society, but to embody, communicate and apply it. The Bible provides instruction on what constitutes right relationships and a relational paradigm for social order.[4] We are called into our full humanity and into a life of service for our fellow human beings, and creation. We vote, not simply for what is best for us, but for what is best for others.

Given all this, *Votewise Now!* presupposes that citizens, particularly Christians, should be actively involved in political issues. This is especially so as we near a national election, hence the timing of this publication. This is the second edition of *Votewise*. The first, written by Nick Spencer, was produced for the 2005 national election. In 2009, the political and social terrain looks decidedly different. Most notably, the current economic crisis and the ensuing recession are set to dominate the next election. Thus, the Jubilee Centre has updated *Votewise* to assist and motivate Christians to respond in the contemporary milieu.

Why Votewise?

Harold Wilson famously said, 'A week is a long time in politics.' The political terrain is dynamic, and necessarily so, and will inevitably change between the completion of this book and the election. However, much of the challenge of *Votewise Now!* is to consider the bigger questions, the underlying values and philosophies that underpin and inform the debate.

The format of this edition is somewhat different from the first. Rather than being written by one author, it is a collection of essays written by informed and engaged experts in their subjects: people who are seeking to integrate their Christian faith with their everyday lives and work. Each essay follows, implicitly or explicitly, the structure: a biblical paradigm, the current debate and a Christian response. The chapters are necessarily limited in scope; owing to space restrictions not every important issue can be included. The essays are not the final or definitive word on any issue, neither do they provide a comprehensive analysis or offer *the* theological approach. They seek to stimulate the reader to think and enquire further, to join up faith and practice, and to provoke preliminary questions that the reader can take forward in their local communities, and to their local and national politicians. To assist this process, each chapter includes a list of further reading material and resources. Needless to say, each chapter has been written from the perspective of the individual author. A short biography of each author is included at the beginning of his or her chapter to help readers better situate them.

The subjects included were chosen for their relevance to today's voters. They impact everyday living, and their potential to shape, improve or disrupt our lives should not be underestimated. Each subject, while dealt with separately, is inevitably interconnected with the rest – which is why a single-issue focus often creates more problems than solutions.

Though many of the contributors will support a particular political party, they have not sought to persuade the reader to vote as they do. We felt therefore that it was important and fair to conclude the book with overt party pitches, each by a committed Christian from one of the three main parties arguing why Christians should support their party. There are committed Christians in each of the three main parties, and each party has an active Christian organization. Much of the disagreement between Christian MPs is about the means rather than the ends – not whether but how to apply their faith. Readers are almost certain to disagree with some of what they say, but we trust that this section will be helpful and thought-provoking.

Some readers may be offended by the focus on the three main parties. However, the fourth-largest party is in fact the Democratic Unionist Party with nine seats, which only operates in

Northern Ireland. The SNP has seven Westminster seats and Plaid Cymru has three. There are a number of other small parties and independents. Though these parties have at times swung significant votes, and may play an important role in a hung Parliament, it is simply not possible to lay out their positions on each issue. That said, the manifestos of these parties can and should be tested against the principles and ideas set out by our contributors.

The political landscape

We are in a recession and the IMF has predicted it may last longer in the UK than in any of the world's other major economies.[5] The financial crisis has raised serious questions about capitalism. Even the *Financial Times* has run a series entitled 'The Future of Capitalism'. The polling company Ipsos MORI regularly asks voters what they consider to be the most important issues facing Britain today. Over the past few years the economy has lagged behind issues such as crime, race relations, the National Health Service (NHS), foreign policy, education and even social security. In January 2008, 20 per cent of voters thought the economy was either the most, or one of the most, important issues. Within a year, that figure had shot up to 70 per cent. That said, polls indicate that other issues such as crime, race relations, unemployment, health care, tax, education, foreign policy, housing and the environment have consistently concerned voters. The economy affects many of these issues, and it is these interactions that will concern most voters.

The economic crisis will significantly impact the next election. The government may hope that the recovery will begin before they must call the election so that they can claim to have saved the country from a global crisis. The Conservatives argue that the UK was ill-prepared for the crisis and that the government is largely to blame for failing to fix the roof while the sun was shining. The Liberal Democrats insist that only Vince Cable saw this crisis coming and that they should therefore be trusted to lead the recovery.

Despite the Liberal Democrats' claim, few really saw the crisis coming on the scale on which it has been experienced. While blame will inevitably play a part in the election, the party which can articulate a credible alternative has the most to gain.

The political compass

The political compass (see Figure 1) is often used to explain and label political thought. It is descriptive, not prescriptive. The parties have moved significantly over the past 30 years and will continue to do so. As the election approaches, they will have to address big issues, changing their position on the compass. Will they spend more on a range of public services? If so, which ones, and how will they pay for this spending – increased debt or higher taxes? If they take on more debt, what are the real costs and who actually pays? If they propose to raise taxes, how much will they go up and who will have to pay them? If they plan to spend less, where will they make the cuts? Will they use the savings to pay off debt or to reduce taxes? If they plan on redu-

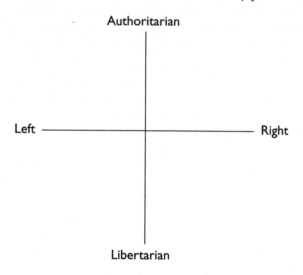

Figure 1: The political compass

cing taxes, which ones and who will benefit? While there are areas of consensus, dividing lines remain on taxation, spending, welfare reform, education and the economy. There is some dispute about the ends to be sought, but much of the disagreement is about the means of getting there. Only in the final stages before an election do the parties set out their detailed proposals. Even then, parties can have a manifesto, but executing it is a different matter.

Left or right?

On the traditional left–right political spectrum, which deals primarily with economic issues, confusion arises because all the parties now occupy the same space. Blair and Brown fought hard in 1995 to persuade the Labour Party to abandon Clause IV, which advocated ownership by the state of the means of production, distribution and exchange. Instead, the Labour government sought much greater public–private partnership and introduced market conditions into parts of the education and health-care system. In 2005 Gordon Brown promised the Confederation of British Industry (CBI) light-touch regulation, saying there would be 'no inspection without justification, no form filling without justification, and no information requirements without justification, not just a light touch, but a limited touch'.[6] At the 2008 Labour Party Conference the Prime Minister proclaimed, 'We are, we always have been and we always will be a pro business government.'

The recession of the early 1990s was followed by 63 consecutive quarters of economic growth,[7] much of it presided over by Gordon Brown as Chancellor. Many did well during the good times, and government figures suggest that 1.8 million children were lifted out of absolute poverty and 600,000 out of relative poverty. However, the gap between rich and poor has stayed remarkably consistent and the UK remains one of the most unequal countries in the developed world.[8]

During this 'boom' period debt spiralled out of all control. Everyone, politicians and voters alike, (literally) bought into a debt-based economy. In response to this 'debt disaster' the Prime Minister wants to see an increased role for the state. His solution to the crisis is a fiscal stimulus and 'quantitative easing' – in short, borrowing (and creating) more to spend more. Similarly in the USA, President Obama is proposing a 'big state' solution. The Conservatives have long been seen as the party of capitalism. However, when David Cameron addressed the World Economic Forum in Davos in 2009, a section of his speech was entitled 'Broken Capitalism'.[9] Having won the battle to be the dominant system of thought, capitalism is now in need of repair. Cameron has explicitly acknowledged a problem with unregulated capitalism and is advocating 'compassionate conservatism/capitalism'. His party wants to reduce the role of the state and encourage the role of society and the voluntary sector. Their inclination is to cut taxes, but in the short term this may not be possible due to the scale of national debt. The Liberal Democrats concede that the state will have to play a larger role in the short term, but believe that the centralization of political and economic power has been part of the problem and that dispersing power is crucial. They want more local banks, more employee-owned companies and fairer taxes paid by everyone.

Biblical economics

Financial policy provides a good example of how the Bible points the way but does not directly indicate how we should vote. Wealth creation is part of the biblical vision for society, but *how* it is attained is the critical issue, not by any means to the detriment of our relationship with God and our neighbour. Capitalism depends on creative destruction, the ongoing replacement of today's objects by tomorrow's 'superior' ones. We are encouraged to consume more and more in an effort to catch up with the dream held out to us. In so doing we spend well into our future, hoping that we can grasp something of its 'reality' today. Capitalism has developed into an impersonal, faceless, largely unquestioned ideology. Everything, from education to health care, is measured, valued and governed according to these principles. Yet there is an argument that capitalism is working well, as the markets have now been forced to correct their earlier exuberance. In biblical terms this could be seen as a period of enforced Jubilee (see Leviticus 25; 26.27–35), the natural consequences of our long-standing Jubilee neglect.

Capitalism's objective is maximization of wealth. As economist Paul Williams has put it, capitalism wants the biggest cake, socialism is concerned with how the cake is divided, but Christianity is interested in how the cake is made. The biblical economic vision is personal, relational and concerned with the creation and preservation of shalom for all.

Where, then, are the modern-day prophets who can imagine an alternative way that will allow Christians to live into their responsibilities as God's chosen people, a light and means of blessing to the nations? This prophetic imagination will serve not only to critique the prevailing state of affairs but also to offer hope for the future in a time of crisis.

The economic crisis has put capitalism to the test and forced the political parties to articulate a new economic vision for the future. We must watch for the party that takes seriously 'how the cake is made', valuing people and imagining a new economic order which promotes relationships.

Top down or bottom up?

In recent years the parties have coalesced around the same economic space, leading to complaints that there is no difference between them. The *24th British Social Attitudes Report*, published in January 2008, suggested that left- and right-wing values are losing their distinctiveness. It concluded that a person's views of left–right issues are now a much less powerful predictor of whether or not they will vote Conservative or Labour.

The authoritarian–libertarian spectrum is often displayed as a vertical axis, with those who favour strict obedience to authority at the top, and those who favour individual freedom at the bottom. The issues related to the authoritarian–libertarian spectrum are of growing importance to voters. The *Faith in the Future* report by a cross-party group of Christian MPs noted the importance of social issues: 'In our understandable pursuit of economic growth we have prejudiced – even sacrificed – our commitment to relationships, care for the local and global environment, transparency in our institutions, respect for each other and the education for a good life.'[10] More questions are now being asked about the focused pursuit of economic goals, but the social sphere is where the dividing lines between the parties are perhaps clearest.

The Liberal Democrat Party, with its strong focus on the individual and civil liberties, is the most libertarian party, though it has recently moved towards the middle. The Conservative Party, with its focus on family, community and voluntary organizations, occupies a slightly authoritarian position. The party has moved closer to the centre under the leadership of David Cameron. The Labour Party, with its focus on state-led solutions, is the most authoritarian, and has become more so in recent years.

Labour, emboldened by President Obama's spending plans, have advocated a stronger role for the state in response to the economic crisis. They have increased spending on areas such as health and education over recent years and will continue as public finances allow. Through tax credits, the minimum wage and welfare-to-work programmes, they have sought to raise the income of the poorest in society. They plan to build more Sure Start Children's Centres and make available more nursery places for younger children. They remain committed to ending child poverty by 2020, though key targets have been missed.

The Conservatives have put a great deal of effort into re-branding themselves. Their main aims are to give people more opportunity and power over their lives, to make families stronger and society more responsible, and to make Britain safer and greener. The Centre for Social Justice, along with other organizations, has raised the profile of social issues within the party. Progressive or compassionate conservatism seeks to pursue social justice and social mobility by conservative means. It will promote the role of mediating institutions such as families, charities, neighbourhoods and co-operatives – the 'little platoons' – which stand between the state and the individual. The Conservatives' desire is for smaller government, but a more vibrant and effective social sphere.

The Liberal Democrats promote social liberalism. Their ideology is 'power to the people'. They emphasize the protection of civil liberties and are adamantly opposed to ID cards and the retention of the DNA records of people with no criminal record. They would scrap council tax and replace it with a local income tax and return business rates to local control. They strongly favour proportional representation. The Liberal Democrats would like the UK to take the lead on nuclear disarmament and increase spending on meeting Millennium Development Goals. They are also strong supporters of the environment, oppose tuition fees, and were against the war in Iraq.

Conclusion

The economic crisis is a chance for everyone to stop and take stock. We as voters should persuade our politicians to adopt the 'triple test' – the idea that policy, legislation and government action should all be subject to economic, environmental and social tests.[11] The economic test has long dominated political debate, and will continue to do so in the current climate, and so 'The Economy' is the first chapter of this book. Recently, policymakers have begun to move towards a second test by recognizing the importance of the environment. However, the biblical text advocates that we need to go even further, and add a neglected third element – the social test, the effect on relationships. This would lead to 'joined-up' public policy, building true national wealth. Such an integrated approach enables politicians and voters alike to take a long-term view, in the better interests of society as a whole.

Notes

1 <www.christiansinpolitics.org.uk/about.htm> (accessed 26 March 2009).
2 Tony Blair, speaking in the documentary *The Blair Years*, 2007.
3 <www.esrcsocietytoday.ac.uk/ESRCInfoCentre/PO/releases/2009/march/politics.aspx?ComponentId=31153&SourcePageId=96> (accessed 26 March 2009).
4 See M. Schluter and J. Ashcroft (eds), *Jubilee Manifesto* (Nottingham: InterVarsity Press, 2005), especially chapter 1.
5 <http://news.bbc.co.uk/1/hi/business/7949978.stm>.
6 <www.hm-treasury.gov.uk/better_regulation_action_plan.htm> (accessed 20 April 2009).
7 <www.statistics.gov.uk/statbase/tsdtables1.asp?vlnk=pn2>, Chained volume measures: seasonally adjusted (accessed 16 April 2009).
8 <www.guardian.co.uk/society/2008/oct/22/equality-wealth-uk-social-mobility> (accessed 1 April 2009).
9 <http://conservativehome.blogs.com/torydiary/files/davidcameronsdavosspeech.pdf> (accessed 9 June 2009).
10 Alistair Burt MP, Andy Reed MP, Caroline Spelman MP, Gary Streeter MP and Steve Webb MP, *Faith in the Future*, 2008, p. 10, available at: <http://campaigndirector.moodia.com/Client/Theos/Files/FITFreport.pdf> (accessed 9 June 2009).
11 *The Triple Test*, The Relationships Foundation, November 2008: <www.relationshipsfoundation.org/thetripletest> (accessed 9 June 2009).

1

The Economy

PAUL WILLIAMS

Paul Williams is Professor of Marketplace Theology and Leadership, and
Executive Director, Regent College Marketplace Institute, Vancouver.
He is also a Director and Economic Adviser to DTZ plc, a multinational
real estate consulting and investment banking group headquartered in
London, for which he has worked extensively throughout Europe, Asia and
North America. Paul graduated from Oxford University with first and
Master's degrees in Economics and Philosophy. He also holds a Master's
degree in Theology from Regent College. He has over 18 years' experience
acting as a strategic economic adviser to a wide range of major international
companies and British and international government departments and
agencies, particularly in the areas of competitiveness, globalization
and sustainability.

The economy is likely to dominate the next election for reasons
good and bad. The 'good' reasons relate to the opportunity to
rethink what we are doing: evidence of major problems in the
economy are all around us thanks to the recession and indebted-
ness left in the wake of the sub-prime crisis in the international
financial system that engulfed the British economy – so let's turn
crisis into opportunity. The 'bad' reasons why the economy is
likely to dominate election discussion is that, too often, we
expect the economy to give us things that it can't give and that
we should look for elsewhere.

It is impossible to do justice to the complexity of economic
issues in a few pages. Instead, this chapter will focus on some
simple questions to help provide a basis for evaluating the political debate on the economy in all its detail. The first question is

simply: What is the economy for? What is its purpose? Why did God create a world in which we both need and enjoy to work together to live? The second question follows on from this: What is it about the economy – the way we do this – that matters to God, and why? While answering these questions won't help us decide whether taxes should be raised or lowered, it may help give some answer to the question of what we should be trying to achieve by raising or lowering taxes.

The biblical paradigm for the economy begins with the command to humanity to 'work' and 'take care' of the Garden of Eden. In the theological orientation of Genesis, the whole of creation is presented as God's temple in which every member of humanity is his image. The Hebrew words used to describe work carry the sense of service and of guarding and keeping something precious. They are the same words used to describe the work of the Levitical priesthood in the tabernacle. The theological point is that work is a co-operative activity of human beings undertaken as an act of worship in God's temple. The root Greek word for the English word 'economics' captures this well – it refers to the stewardship of a household. Economics is fundamentally humanity's stewardship of God's creation 'household'.

The Bible then, has a very high view of work. It is one of the primary ways in which we image God. We work because God works, co-creating with him in his purposes in creation, and we work in community as a reflection of God's Trinitarian nature. Overall, work is a place of creativity, enterprise and delight as we collaborate to celebrate and honour God in the way we partner with him to govern, magnify and adorn creation. That is what the economy is for.

The impact of the Fall is that our work tends to be idolatrous rather than worshipful, selfish rather than co-operative, exploitative rather than caring of creation. This is the context in which God has to teach us how he wants us to work together. After the Fall, God emphasizes certain limits on economic activity designed to highlight care (for creation and people), limiting the damage of the Fall on the economy, and orienting our economic life towards community and God's original purpose. In the Old Testament, every family group is given some land to steward – a small piece of creation in which they have the opportunity to offer work as worship to God. Any surplus produced beyond their own needs could be exchanged in the market. There is private property, but with some important differences. First, it is far less individualistic – much property ownership in Israel is deliberately structured familially, not individually. Second, ownership is not absolute. God reminds Israel that ultimately he owns both the land and the people, and they cannot be treated like commodities. Land can only be leased, not sold, and must be given a Sabbath rest. People must not be permanently enslaved or indebted. The things that are produced through work – food, clothing and other goods – are not to be thought of as mine in an absolute sense, but as gifts entrusted to me for the benefit of others.

The biblical vision is that co-operative worshipful work is the basic modus operandi of life on earth and nobody should be excluded from the opportunity to enter into it. Economic injustice occurs when we move away from an economy of mutual dependence and care towards one of autonomy and power. Two major theological motifs that run right throughout Scripture reinforce this overall message. The Sabbath is both a limit on work, expressing care for people and the land, and a celebration of life together – not simply a time to recover so we can work again the following week. Similarly, the Jubilee institutions impose limits that are supposed to act as a failsafe, giving everyone a fresh start so that each generation has the opportunity to live obediently and abundantly. No wonder that Jesus was willing to offend the Pharisees by celebrating life on the Sabbath and adopted the Jubilee as the definition of his own ministry (Luke 4.14–21, quoting Isaiah 61).

These themes develop throughout both Testaments. In the New Testament, Christians are again called in Christ to work together with God, undertaking work he has 'prepared in advance for us to do' (Ephesians 2.10). By the Spirit we are enabled to work with God as he renews creation and restores all things in Christ (Ephesians 1.10). We tend to spiritualize these words so that they only refer to certain 'sacred' activities, but the Bible teaches that when God lays claim to 'all things' he really does mean all things, including our work as accountants, cleaners and pastry chefs. Sabbath and Jubilee find their ultimate consummation in God's kingdom, in which we enter God's rest and shalom – the profound peace that comes when all our relationships are rightly ordered. Amazingly, the potential for all our work of human culture-building is that it be included in the worship offered to God in the New Jerusalem (see Revelation 21.26).

The contrast between this vision and that of contemporary economic life in Britain is startling. To begin with, work is often regarded as a necessary evil rather than as a delight. Many people live for the weekend when they can stop work and consume, so work is reduced to simply a rather stressful but unavoidable means of making money for oneself. Economists also model work in this way – as a 'disutility' that people will only pursue if paid to do so. This has the result of narrowing the scope of what we often mean by 'work' to paid employment, rendering much purposeful and honouring work undertaken by volunteers, family members or the disabled as somehow 'second class'.

Furthermore, the amount of work that we do is often out of balance. At one extreme, a growing number are out of work as a result of the current recession. More than 2 million people are officially unemployed and this number is expected to grow to around 3 million by early 2010 – numbers we have not seen since the early 1980s. At another extreme, we all know that those who are workaholics seem unable to stop pursuing more achievement, more money and are simply so fearful of losing out that they cannot rest. Finally, most of us, even if we enjoy work most of the time, find workplaces increasingly pressurizing and stressful environments. The overall effect is that too often work feels less of a creative delight and more like a treadmill: lots of activity going nowhere in particular.

All this activity is driven by our focus on economic growth; that is, our unwillingness to accept limits on our economic activity. We have bought into the myth that more money and more things will make us happy. This idea is built into modern capitalism and economic policy. In a completely deregulated market – so the argument goes – individuals will be free to exercise choice in pursuit of their vision of happiness, and the price system will enable all of these different individual preferences to be co-ordinated so that society as a whole is as happy as possible. Economic growth, in this view, is somehow a proxy or measure of happiness, and therefore to be pursued. Anything that restricts the operation of markets will reduce choice and reduce market efficiency and so reduce economic growth. This logic is what lies behind economic policies to deregulate markets of all kinds: whether for labour (for example, this is why Britain has been so resistant to European Union (EU) limitations on working time), capital (for example, this explains the reluctance to regulate debt or limit speculative capital flows), or goods and services (for example, this is why Sunday trading restrictions have been lifted). We need to be clear that the modern resistance to any kind of limitation on the market stands in direct opposition to God's insistence that economic activity recognizes limits of care for both people and creation.

Our pursuit of growth has become an addiction, most obvious in the mountain of debt owed by Britons on credit cards and personal loans, let alone the mortgage debt that has ballooned in part because many have withdrawn equity from their houses in order to finance further consumption. *Votewise* sounded the alarm on high debt levels ahead of the last election. Since then, household debt servicing costs – the amount spent repaying debt – has risen as a percentage of disposable income from 18 per cent in 2005 to nearly 25 per cent at the end of 2008. Lower interest rates in 2009 should help reduce this figure slightly, but the point remains that Britons are astonishingly burdened by debt, even compared with nations like the USA, where debt servicing costs stand at around 14 per cent. Economic life in contemporary

Britain is characterized more by stress, addictive craving and greed than by delight, contentment and care. One commentator rather aptly describes this kind of 'growth' as 'cancerous' – multiplication as an end in itself which threatens the health of the whole society.

The current economic crisis is best understood, then, not as a problem caused by defaults on sub-prime loans – these defaults were simply the straw that broke the camel's back – but rather as the result of a 30-year rise in debt levels throughout British society. These high debt levels mean that the current recession is likely to be particularly painful since with high levels of debt and low savings, job losses are far more likely to convert into personal bankruptcy and homelessness. There is an incredible irony in this situation. After all, isn't capitalism's promise that through the exercise of personal freedom of choice in the market we will achieve progress and somehow enter our future? Capitalism promised us this freedom yet it has led instead to stagnation, despair and, ultimately, increasing enslavement. The fundamental reason for this is that modern capitalism has focused on the wrong goal for economic life – maximizing growth and profit – and as a result has eroded its own moral, social and relational foundation, actively encouraging selfish and greedy behaviour that has ended up causing a great deal of damage to large numbers of people.

So how do we respond to all of this? It is salutary to consider that the primary two reasons given by the Old Testament prophets for Israel's exile from the land were idolatry and socio-economic injustice. In our pursuit of wealth and material things at the expense of other people and creation, are we not sinning in exactly the same ways? God's reaction to Israel was grief and anger, and these emotions led to three main kinds of action: first, prophetic speech and warning; second, judgement; and third, comfort, mercy and messages of hope. Perhaps a Christian response to the present state of our social and economic life should be characterized in these same ways. What might that look like?

First, we should not shy away from speaking up about these issues. In particular, we should 'speak up for those who cannot speak for themselves' (Proverbs 31.8–9), like the small-firm owners or newly jobless families who suddenly find their modest supply of debt cut off by a bank that was previously all too happy to throw as much debt at them as possible, but now is willing to see them go bankrupt or to repossess their house. In the midst of a popular 'witch hunt' against investment bankers, we should also not allow politicians to evade their own responsibility for allowing the huge build-up in debt that they profited from via taxation and faster economic 'growth'.

In addition to speaking out on particular issues of oppression or need, we can also confront the basic idolatry that underlies our pursuit of economic growth – after all, we can't simply blame bankers and politicians for all the debt we've got into as a society. Unfortunately, the reality is that none of the major political parties in Britain depart in any meaningful way from the basic assumption that we should pursue economic growth and that more material wealth will make us 'better off'. One of the most effective things Christians can do in this election is to start to shift the terms of the debate by asking hard questions about why we are pursuing this goal when we know it doesn't make us happier and in fact is causing environmental and social damage. A classic defence of economic growth is that without it we can't help the poor, but that of course both ignores the real limits on growth and the way in which our current system enables the rich to extract a hugely disproportionate share of national wealth. Steady-state economies are perfectly viable (and can be full of enterprise, innovation and creativity) but they don't need debt creation to survive. Growth via massive debt creation has an inbuilt bias to the rich because it is the wealthy who can access debt the quickest, in the largest quantities and at the lowest cost. Think about housing as an example: those who can access the cheapest mortgage finance can outbid others and then use the artificial asset price increase to pay off the real value of the debt they have borrowed. Meanwhile, those who can't access debt find that house prices keep moving further and further away from their reach.

Second, so far as justice is concerned, God reserves acts of judgement to himself and to the state. We should expect our political leaders, therefore, to act to put right some of the wrongs that have occurred in the economy. God's particular anger is directed at leaders responsible for either exploiting people or leading them astray. In the former category we might insist that politicians prevent lenders from now oppressing those struggling to repay debts. This particularly applies to banks now in public ownership/control or in receipt of public 'bailouts'. In the latter category we should certainly include those lenders encouraging their customers to take on higher and higher levels of debt, and regulators, including politicians themselves, who actively permitted the huge climb in debt levels or who kept insisting that economic growth is an imperative, despite repeated warnings from some economists and social commentators. Many other particular issues – such as the corrosive effect of advertising, the favourable tax treatment of debt and advertising in corporate accounts, or the ability of shareholders to pressurize banks and other firms to maximize their profits but then evade responsibility for the impact of these activities on society – are all explored in more detail than space permits discussion of here on the Jubilee Centre website: <www.jubilee-centre.org>.

In all this, one tendency we need to avoid is that of the dominant response to the current crisis, namely that we now need the state to save us from the mess we're in. While there is certainly a need for wise governance to help us respond appropriately, there is a huge danger in thinking that the solution is simply more regulation and state intervention in the market. Our tendency here is to expect the state to act as the conscience of society as a replacement for the moral responsibility that we as individual citizens have failed to exercise. This will only lead to more enslavement in the end.

Finally, God's care, mercy and messages of hope are given now primarily through and in the life of the Church, not the state. Increasingly, we need to recover an understanding of how the Church in its corporate life is supposed to function as an alternative political body within society, witnessing to the very different citizenship that we have in heaven. Can we as the Church embody in our life together something that looks a lot more like the biblical paradigm? A life characterized by Sabbath and Jubilee would be one that celebrated our relational life together in God's presence and from which we acted to see the oppressed, indebted and addicted freed. Above all, our corporate life should be one in which our desire for God eclipses and purifies any idolatrous desire for the material goals of our society. Our actions would then be motivated by a real sense of grief and anger as we learn to share and carry God's heart for the world, including in our engagement with the upcoming election.

Further engaging

Publications

Daniel M. Bell, Jr, 'What is Wrong with Capitalism? The Problem with the Problem with Capitalism'; and William Cavanaugh, 'Consumption, the Market and the Eucharist', in *The Other Journal* (<www.theotherjournal.com>)

William T. Cavanaugh, *Being Consumed: Economics and Christian Desire* (Grand Rapids: Eerdmans, 2008)

Darrell Cosden, *A Theology of Work: Work and the New Creation* (Paternoster Theological Monographs, 2006)

Milton Friedman, *Capitalism and Freedom* (Chicago: University of Chicago Press, 1962)

Donald Hay, *Economics Today: A Christian Critique* (Nottingham: InterVarsity Press/Apollos and Vancouver: Regent College Publishing, 1989)

Gordon Wenham, *Genesis* (Word Biblical Commentary, 1987)

Stefan Cardinal Wyszynski, *All You Who Labor: Work and the Sanctification of Daily Life* (Manchester, NH: Sophia Press, 1995)

2

Criminal Justice

JONATHAN BURNSIDE

Dr Jonathan Burnside is Reader in Biblical Law at the School of Law, University of Bristol. He spearheaded the 'Relational Justice' project for the Jubilee Centre. His work explores the relationship between law, theology and criminology from theoretical and applied perspectives and his books include *The Signs of Sin: Seriousness of Offence in Biblical Law* (2003), and *My Brother's Keeper: Faith-based Units in Prisons* (2005), as well as a forthcoming book on biblical law, provisionally entitled *God, Justice and Society*.

Introduction

It's a summer evening and you're sitting outside in your garden when all of a sudden you hear a crash and a tinkle of glass. Someone has just thrown a bottle of beer through your greenhouse, smashing several panes. You phone the police to complain. A little while later your next-door neighbour comes round. It turns out that his son has had a few friends round for a party, things got a bit out of hand and a beer bottle was thrown onto your greenhouse. He's very sorry about it and will come round to pay for the damage (just as soon as he gets over his hangover). You say that's fine and get back to the garden. Five minutes later, the doorbell rings again. It's the police, come to investigate a complaint about criminal damage. You explain that's it all been sorted out and there's no need to press charges. But the police aren't interested. They've lots of performance targets to hit, including crimes to detect, charge, process and clear up. It's in their interest to obtain a conviction, regardless of what you have been able to sort out with the miscreant.

Some recent trends in criminal justice

It's only a random snapshot, of course, but one that sums up a number of recent trends in criminal justice. We've come to see justice in increasingly managerial terms. Criminal justice is seen as a service, like health and education, the function of which is to serve customers in the form of victims and witnesses. One of the results is that 'doing justice' is increasingly defined in terms of prosecuting and punishing more people. Accordingly, since 1997, we have had more than 50 pieces of criminal justice legislation and more than 3,000 new criminal offences. It is part of a consumerist approach to justice which holds that we increase the quantum of justice by making it easier to prosecute and punish more people. That's part of the reason why your damaged greenhouse is processed – even though it is not a particularly sensible or a relational response – because the government has a target to increase the number of 'offences brought to justice' (OBTJs). Justice is said to be delivered in increasingly target-oriented terms. But is there not more to justice than this?

One of the consequences of this approach is that more and more people are caught up in the criminal justice process for less and less serious offences. In 2006 Rod Morgan (the then-Chair of the Youth Justice Board) claimed that between 35,000 and 40,000 young people were being prosecuted in front of magistrates when ten years ago they were dealt with outside the formal court system. We're also putting more of them in custody than ever before. A 2008 report from the British Children's Commissioners to the United Nations Committee on the Rights of the Child shows that the UK now locks up more children than any other Western European country, even though the number of crimes committed by children fell between 2002 and 2006.

The same trend towards large-scale penal containment can also be seen in regard to adults. When the Jubilee Centre first started work on these issues in 1991 the prison population in England and Wales stood at 36,000. It currently stands at 82,000 (as of January 2009). This is an increase of about 130 per cent.

Previously, it took about 40 years for the prison population to increase by 25,000 (between 1958 and 1995). How much is enough? Especially when all this is happening at a time when the British Crime Survey and police statistics indicate that most crime rates have been falling.

Perhaps the best reason for these developments is that, regardless of what the official figures may show, fear of crime is rising. Underlying our perceptions of a 'safe' society is our sense of the quality of our relationships in civic society. Compared to previous decades we are feeling less connected than ever before. Studies show that even the strongest community today is weaker than the weakest community a generation ago. Many of us do not know who our neighbours are and we are simply not used to sorting things out at a local level. This has a bearing on the greenhouse example. If we had better relationships with our neighbours, we might not have been on the phone so quickly to the police in the first place.

Clearly, issues around crime and social disorder demand a complex and multifaceted response. And since we obviously haven't got all the answers, we may as well ask whether ideas about justice found in the Bible might be a place from which we can take our bearings as we struggle with these questions. And we find – perhaps to the surprise of those who have only seen biblical justice in terms of 'an eye for an eye and a tooth for a tooth' – that the Bible provides us with an inspiring vision that encourages us to think about justice in terms of relationships.

A brief overview of justice and punishment in the Bible

The starting point for understanding justice in the Bible is God, because justice is a characteristic of God and he is the source of it all (Deuteronomy 32.4). This means that knowledge of justice is relational, not simply propositional. And because justice is a characteristic of God himself, it is inseparable from God's other characteristics, including his kindness, his love and his righteousness (which encompasses a concern for 'right relationships').

Consequently, justice in the Bible always takes sides when it comes to good and evil. It upholds what God defines as 'good' and opposes what God defines as 'evil' (although of course God's justice is impartial so far as the identities of the parties are concerned, for example Deuteronomy 10.17–18).

If true justice upholds good and opposes evil, it follows that there are two sides to justice in the Bible. On the one hand, justice brings down the oppressor and on the other hand it liberates the oppressed. So biblical justice has very different consequences and can be experienced very differently depending on which side you happen to fall on (e.g. Psalm 146.7–9). The same act of justice brings oppressors 'to ruin' and 'lifts up those who are bowed down'.

Accordingly, the greatest example of God's justice in the Old Testament (judging oppressors, liberating the weak) is the Exodus from Egypt. Here, God destabilized the totalitarian rule of Pharaoh in order to deliver the descendants of Abraham from slavery. Similarly, the greatest example of God's justice in the New Testament is the crucifixion of Jesus – an event that is expressly characterized as the 'new Exodus' (Luke 9.31, where Jesus' 'departure', or 'exodus' in the Greek, refers to his crucifixion). The New Testament understands the cross as a new and better Exodus because it overthrows a greater oppressor than Pharaoh and liberates a greater number of people (see Hebrews 3—4). For Jesus, the real oppressor of Israel was not the Romans but the Accuser, Satan. Paul describes this greatest act of salvation as a manifestation of God's justice (Romans 3.25–26). The cross is the ultimate act of God's justice in the Bible because it overthrows the ultimate oppressor and bestows the ultimate freedom from tyranny (Hebrews 2.15–16; Romans 8.14–17). The Last Judgement is an act of divine justice that finally brings the victory of Israel's Messiah on the cross to bear eternally upon the whole of creation. There is eternal retribution and eternal restoration. Everything that oppresses God's creation is overthrown, and everything that seeks freedom from bondage is fully liberated. Again, the picture of what it means for us to be in partnership with God and to seek divine justice will mean challenging evil and overthrowing oppression in many different forms and also about liberating the oppressed. For these reasons, biblical justice is transformative. It is a saving action by God that puts things right, and this is reflected in biblical images of justice. Amos declared 'let justice roll down like waters, and righteousness like an ever-flowing stream' (Amos 5.24, NRSV). Justice is here seen as a mighty, surging river, like the Jordan in full flood. This picture teaches us that justice is not a static state (like the scales of Justicia) but an intervening power: it strikes and changes, restores and heals. It's dynamic and it rushes onwards and it brings life to a parched land. Justice has the potential to be transformative, not only to the victim of the crime but also to the offender. Indeed, there are some cases when it can be quite difficult to tell the difference between the victim and the perpetrator. Often offenders themselves are subject to oppression of various kinds and they too are in need of liberation.

It also means that justice is relational because it is always concerned with fulfilling the rightful demands of a given relationship. This is why justice and righteousness (understood in terms of 'right relationships') always go together because the righteous person is the person who fulfils the specific demands of a given relationship. This has important implications. To punish with justice means that it is not enough simply to punish. Justice is not served simply by punishing people but by putting things right.

Pursuing justice was meant to be a national priority for biblical Israel. Justice is not a luxury, or an optional extra, but a means to life (Deuteronomy 16.20). At the same time, it is something that is hard to achieve and requires our 'hot pursuit' (the meaning of the word 'follow' in verse 20). According to the Bible, laying hold of justice is something that we learn to do as we grow in wisdom and character (see Exodus 18.21 and Proverbs 9.10). It is for this reason that the content and application of biblical law, both in terms of its substantive and procedural aspects, have much in common with wisdom.

Do we want a culture of control or a relational society?

If justice in the Bible is characterized by a concern for relationships and transformation, then part of the answer might be to think relationally about criminal justice, all the way from social breakdown through crime prevention and policing to sentencing, incarceration and resettlement. In other words, we try to close the so-called 'justice gap', not by making it easier to prosecute and punish more people, but by being concerned with right relationships at every level. We develop our policies by asking at every stage, what is the likely impact of this or that policy on the quality of relationships within the criminal justice process? The relational question needs to be asked because justice is transformative and not a static state. Doing justice means making room for growth, healing and the possibility of restored relationships. It is integral to punishing with justice. If this question isn't asked, punishment loses its legitimacy and moral authority.

Obviously, in this short account, we can't look at all the different aspects of something as complex as the criminal justice process. But we can highlight three large areas that need to be addressed.

First, our tolerance of the large numbers of people we send to custody and the quality of their regimes. Most prisoners today face a 'regime of eventlessness and a life that is redundant, monotonous and stultifying . . . programmes that offer an opportunity to contribute to the world are virtually non-existent'.[1] There is a need to develop more active prison regimes, and especially regimes that encourage prisoner responsibility.[2] But to do this effectively there needs to be a collective determination to reduce the use of imprisonment. This is perfectly reasonable because there's good evidence that, in the UK, prison is increasingly being used for reasons not directly linked with crime, or with the reduction of crime, or even with the punishment of crime, but, rather, it is often linked to the control of marginalized and impoverished groups in society. Some other countries, such as Russia, have managed to reduce their levels of imprisonment by 20 per cent, discovering in the process that less criminal justice can lead to more justice.[3]

Second, the assumed role of the state in delivering criminal justice. Massive centralization over the past 20 to 30 years has led us to assume that the state should have a huge role when it comes to criminal justice, but this is a mistake. There is a need to devolve responsibility to citizens, local communities and courts and give them a role in securing justice because the key way we deal with crime is by renewing civic society. The criminal justice process can by itself have only a limited effect on the general level of crime and so action is needed by communities and between individuals as citizens that is beyond the scope and capacity of the statutory criminal justice agencies.

Third, we need to reconnect crime control and criminal justice with broader themes of social justice and social reconstruction.[4] Many of the people who are being brought 'into the net' are people whom the criminal justice process is ill-equipped to deal with. Many have serious relational deficits: it is estimated that 47 per cent of male sentenced prisoners ran away from home as a child, 49 per cent were excluded from school, 72 per cent suffer from two or more mental disorders, 66 per cent used drugs in the previous year, and 67 per cent were unemployed prior to their imprisonment.[5] Nelson Mandela once commented that 'a country should be judged, not by how it treats its highest citizens, but how it treats its lowest ones'. There is a need for 'joined-up' thinking in this area, with criminal justice worked out in regard to family policy, education, housing and employment, among other areas of social policy.

These are all big questions that need to be addressed at the next election. Of course, we may be happy about things the way they are. After all, we may be reaping certain benefits from our current approach, in terms of limited formal control and some sense of security (even if this does not outweigh our current fear of crime). But the problem is that because they are non-relational strategies, they are extremely expensive. Worse, they only encourage us to disengage and slide towards a 'culture of control'. This could be an even costlier problem and an even heavier burden for future generations. It all means that the real question for the next general election is: do we want to create a culture of control, or do we want to build a relational society?

Notes

1   Hans Toch, 'Commonality in Prisons', *Relational Justice Bulletin* 7.1–3, 2000, p. 2, <http://relationshipsfoundation.org/resources/search.php? keyword=relational+justice+bulletin&x=0&y=0&p=26&c=28> (accessed 4 March 2009).

2   Stephen Pryor, *The Responsible Prisoner* (London: HM Inspectorate of Prisons, 2001), <http://inspectorates.homeoffice.gov.uk/hmiprisons/ thematic-reports1/the-responsible-prisoner.pdf> (accessed 4 March 2009).

3   Yuri Ivanovich Kalinin, *The Russian Penal System: Past, Present and Future* (London: International Centre for Prison Studies, 2002), <www.kcl.ac. uk/depsta/law/research/icps/downloads/website%20kalinin.pdf> (accessed 4 March 2009).

4   David Garland, *The Culture of Control: Crime and Social Order in Contemporary Society* (Oxford: Oxford University Press, 2001), p. 199.

5   Social Exclusion Unit, *Reducing Reoffending by Ex-prisoners* (London: Social Exclusion Report, 2002), <www.cabinetoffice.gov.uk/media/ cabinetoffice/social_exclusion_task_force/assets/publications_1997_to_ 2006/reducing_report.pdf> (accessed 4 March 2009).

Further engaging

Publications

Jonathan Burnside, 'Criminal Justice', in Michael Schluter and John Ashcroft (eds), *Jubilee Manifesto* (Nottingham: InterVarsity Press, 2005), pp. 234–54

Jonathan Burnside and Nicola Baker (eds), *Relational Justice: Repairing the Breach* (Winchester: Waterside Press, 1994, reprinted 2004)

Jonathan Burnside, *God, Justice and Society* (forthcoming)

David Garland, *The Culture of Control: Crime and Social Order in Contemporary Society* (Oxford: Oxford University Press, 2001)

Christopher D. Marshall, *Beyond Retribution: A New Testament Vision for Justice, Crime and Punishment* (Grand Rapids, MI: Eerdmans, 2001)

Websites

International Centre for Prison Studies: <www.kcl.ac.uk/schools/law/research/icps>

Prison Reform Trust: <www.prisonreformtrust.org.uk>

The Relationships Foundation: <www.relationshipsfoundation.org>

Relational Justice Bulletin archive: <www.relationshipsfoundation.org/relationaljusticebulletin>

3

Health Care

ANDREW FERGUSSON

Andrew Fergusson worked as a GP in a Christian mission practice in south London for ten years, and for the past twenty has worked at the interface of medicine and Christianity. He is currently Head of Communications at Christian Medical Fellowship.

What is health?

In 2009 the UK will spend around £100 billion on health, and although that money is allocated in advance, a 7 per cent cut is expected in 2010 as the recession impacts health care. Surprisingly, given these huge sums, there has been little serious discussion of what 'health' actually is. It is an important question.

Consideration is usually at two extremes. At one is a minimal biomedical definition: 'the absence of disease or infirmity'. This may fit comfortably with the traditional goal of medicine – after all, doctors define a healthy patient as someone who hasn't been investigated adequately yet! But it takes no account of patients as whole people with psychological, social and spiritual needs, nor of the broader causes of ill health – poverty, poor nutrition, pollution, unhealthy lifestyle, workplace hazards, social isolation, family breakdown, etc.

At the other extreme are maximal holistic definitions, like the World Health Organization's (WHO) 'Health is a state of complete physical, mental and social well-being, not simply the absence of disease or infirmity.' (Interestingly, 50 years after 1948, WHO added the concept of spiritual needs.) However, this definition is far too all-embracing, is unachievably utopian, and the enormous disparities around the world make it sometimes almost offensive to the global needy.

Christians are therefore drawn to the middle ground definition suggested by the theologian Jürgen Moltmann that 'health is the strength to be human'. It is free from Christian jargon, is realistic in that any caring person anywhere in the world can always give another more strength to be more human, and most importantly it raises the following vital question:

What does it mean to be human?

Christians respond above all in terms of relationships: with God, with others, with self and with the environment. And these relationships centre on the unique nature of human beings – unlike all the animals, humans alone are made in the image of God (Genesis 1.26–27). This explains the prohibition later in Genesis on taking the lives of legally innocent humans: 'And from each man, too, I will demand an accounting for the life of his fellow man. Whoever sheds the blood of man, by man shall his blood be shed; for in the image of God has God made man' (9.5–6). While we must argue against abortion and euthanasia in other terms too, for Christians those issues begin here and human uniqueness should remain central in the debates about assisted suicide which will doubtless continue into the next Parliament.

What is health care?

If health concerns the strength to be human, then health care is anything which moves individuals and communities towards having more strength to be more human. Generally, health care is provided by trained professionals, but taking broader holistic views means that non-professionals who may or may not even recognize themselves as 'carers' are involved too. Indeed, health and social services would flounder without the billions of pounds' worth of health care provided by volunteers and lay carers. With the cuts inevitable in the recession, family and community commitment to those in need will be essential.

Are there Christian hallmarks for health care?

Like all parables, the 'Good Samaritan' (Luke 10.25–37) is told to communicate a particular message, and we should beware reading too much into its details. However, only Luke the physician recounts it, and he would surely reference his outlook as a professional. We can therefore legitimately discern a secondary meaning – permanent principles that Luke suggests are hallmarks for health care:

Comprehensive compassion

But a Samaritan . . . took pity on him. (Luke 10.33)

We know nothing about the traveller who has been mugged except that he has been left 'half dead'. By chance a priest comes along, perhaps having done a week's Temple duty serving God. Now he has a chance to serve his fellow man, but famously 'he passed by on the other side'. He may have feared falling victim himself, or becoming ritually defiled by a dead body. We don't know. Likewise, we know no more about the Levite – although his Temple responsibilities may have provided the same excuse.

Jesus has the audience spellbound. Who's going to be the hero? Probably, most are expecting a Jewish layperson, and we would need first-hand experience of ethnic conflict in a divided community to appreciate what follows. When Jesus says, 'But a Samaritan . . .' there would have been outrage. 'Who is my neighbour?' was a common theological debating point, and for the audience 'neighbour' meant at least a fellow Jew or a full convert to Judaism. Pharisees went further and excluded tax collectors and sinners. But that the real hero, the real neighbour, should be a Samaritan . . . !

The Bible's 'took pity' is better translated 'had compassion', and health care must begin with compassion. The English roots mean 'to suffer with' and the word communicates strong internal empathy. For once, 'I feel your pain' would mean what it says! The UK's leading health think-tank, the King's Fund, released a hard-hitting report in December 2008 lamenting the lack of compassion in the NHS, and subsequently launched a pilot 'Point of Care' programme. Its chief executive said:

> Most of us know from our own experience that while care is often fantastic, it is sometimes impersonal and lacks compassion. Yet how we are treated can affect how we recover and for a hospital there is scarcely anything more important than ensuring that every patient is treated with kindness and consideration – not as a collection of symptoms but as an individual with anxieties, feelings and views.

The pilot seeks to determine 'why staff don't always provide the sort of care they would want for themselves and their own families'. Informal soundings suggest that excessive tick-box bureaucracy diverts staff from their preferred priority. It is proposed that large, purpose-built 'polyclinics' will have a wide range of primary and secondary care staff to facilitate prompt referral and specialized treatments. But polyclinics are likely to be impersonal, and because of being sited far from some users, will cause transport difficulties.

The King's Fund experts confirm what many professionals and patients already know – the NHS needs more compassion, more simple, old-fashioned kindness. Compassion, however, must be more than subjective feeling: it must be objective, with a practical outcome. Who do we show compassion to? We show it to our neighbour. And who is my neighbour? Well, that's the whole point of the parable. We must respond to the responsibility placed on us by the need of any other.

The compassion foundational for health care is comprehensive. It cannot be selective. It took a long battle by campaigners, who included Christians, to succeed in 2008 in overturning a government ban on providing primary health care to failed asylum-seekers. It was argued that this ban breached the spirit and the letter of the law, the principles and practice of public health, and professional ethics. Similar issues are likely to recur, and of course desperate global health needs should be a constant challenge.

Costly commitment

He went to him . . . (Luke 10.34)

The Samaritan felt compassion, then 'went to him'. There was a risk that the figure might have been a decoy, intended to lure others into the hands of the muggers, but his compassion led to commitment to action. So, in health care, compassion requires subsequent commitment.

However, it is biblical to recognize and count the cost. Again it is Dr Luke who reports the words of Jesus: 'Suppose one of you wants to build a tower. Will he not first sit down and estimate the cost . . . ?' (Luke 14.28). For individual health professionals, salaries may be much lower than in other walks of life. There will be pressures on family life caused by working hours, and the compulsory response to the European Working Time Directive may require shift-working which is ultimately more stressful. There may be physical risks of acquiring serious or even fatal infection – with uncertainty over how many will be affected by future global pandemics, medical journals are debating the limits to a health professional's responsibility to get involved. During pandemics in the early centuries, the Christians stood out because, rather than leaving the cities, they stayed behind to care for the sick and dying.

And there is a massive financial cost. Will we be able to retain a health service that always provides care free at the point of need? If so, how will we fund it? To what extent will we be prepared to put our money where our mouth is? Is central taxation the best route for financing a recession-restricted NHS? Or should Independent Sector Treatment Centres develop the market for a mixed public–private health service?

If so, would Britain end up with two-tier health care – a higher quality for those who can afford to choose it, and a mere safety net service for those who cannot? Should we continue to build new hospitals via the Private Finance Initiative? That way they get built, on time and within budget, but the state spends the next 25 years paying back with interest the private companies who took the initial risk. What should good stewardship dictate?

And what of the commitment of patients themselves to others? What is the Christian attitude to organ donation? If 'Greater love has no one than this, that he lay down his life for his friends' (John 15.13) then surely altruistic donation of body organs after death is a Christian thing to do? But is 'presumed consent', where the state removes organs at death unless the individual has opted out, the same thing?

Conscientious competence

> . . . and bandaged his wounds, pouring on oil and wine . . .
> (Luke 10.34)

These actions may seem quaint now, but oil and wine then were the definitive treatments. The Samaritan did the best he could, given what he knew, and with the resources available. Resources depend not just on the budgets for health care, but on researching and developing new treatments and continuing to evaluate old ones. Research budgets should be maintained and protected, and Christians should be at the forefront of ensuring that research involves both good ethics and good science.

In stem-cell research and treatment, all the clinical benefits have come from ethically non-controversial adult stem cells, and none at all from controversial human embryonic sources. *Imago Dei* can be respected while ethical science develops effective treatments.

Conscientious competence, regulated ultimately by appropriate statutory but independent bodies, should mark all Christian service: 'Whatever you do, work at it with all your heart, as working for the Lord, not for men . . . It is the Lord Christ you are serving' (Colossians 3.23–24).

Continuing care

Then he put the man on his own donkey, brought him to an inn and took care of him. The next day he took out two silver coins and gave them to the innkeeper. 'Look after him,' he said, 'and when I return, I will reimburse you for any extra expense you may have.' (Luke 10.34–36)

We must not read too much into parables, and cannot base transport, accommodation and fiscal policies for the NHS on this quote! However, continuing care is clearly important. Luke spends more words on chronic care than on the acute situation.

No health manager purchasing care can possibly write blank cheques. Even the richest nations cannot meet all the conceivable costs of continuing care, and, with increasing life expectancy in Britain, prioritizing will become more important than ever. To what extent should individual patients play a greater part as partners in their own health care? Are patient contracts and individual budgets for patients with chronic conditions a good way of handing over responsibility and accountability? Or might patients not have all the knowledge needed to make fully informed choices? Without returning to inappropriate paternalism, how can health professionals in the future best come alongside patients in assuming joint responsibility for costs?

While emergency and acute services are dramatic and glamorous and easy to raise money for, whether in NHS budgets or charitable fundraising, the so-called Cinderella specialties are the opposite. Yet patients in these expanding categories (and probably those with dementia are the most obvious example) matter every bit as much. Down the years Christians have pioneered and maintained service in unpopular specialties, and must continue to do so.

Christ's commendation

Jesus told him, 'Go and do likewise.' (Luke 10.37)

When the legal expert reluctantly had to reply that the Samaritan was the true neighbour, Jesus implicitly commended that example. All involved in health care, whether politician, professional, patient or patient's carer, need to be honest with themselves about motivation. Is it simply to receive Christ's commendation, 'Well done, good and faithful servant!' (Matthew 25.23), or is it to receive acknowledgement, prestige, status, fame and fortune, honorary degrees, a particular office, honours, a knighthood? These rewards may come, but the lure of them can be a snare.

It is said that Mother Teresa did all she did simply because, in the words of Matthew 25.40, 'whatever you did for one of the least of these brothers of mine, you did for me'.

Further engaging

Publications

A. Fergusson, *Hard Questions about Health and Healing* (London: CMF, 2005)

A. Fergusson, 'Hallmarks for Healthcare', *Triple Helix*, Autumn 2000, pp. 14–15

S. Fouch, 'Winning a Care Fight', *Triple Helix*, Christmas 2008, pp. 12–13

Websites

The King's Fund, 'Point of Care': <www.kingsfund.org.uk>

The Christian Medical Fellowship's website has a Christian perspective on most health-care issues: <www.cmf.org.uk>

4

Education

TREVOR COOLING

Trevor Cooling is Director of the 'Transforming Lives' project, an inter-denominational initiative that promotes teaching as a Christian vocation among churches and Christian organizations in the UK. He has over 30 years' education experience as a classroom teacher, Head of Religious Education in a secondary school, chief executive of a Christian education charity, curriculum developer, author, government adviser, university lecturer, and schools adviser for the Diocese of Gloucester. He has a PhD in Religious Education from the University of Birmingham.

Introduction

Probably the simplest, but most challenging, question politicians have to answer in their policy-making is, 'What is education for?' If they cannot answer that, they will not be able to recognize success in schools, colleges and universities. Far too often, they assume the answer is, following Bill Clinton, 'It's the economy, stupid.' But surely the Christian community should seek an education that is built on more than this?

Current British education is, in many ways, stunningly impressive. Today's teachers are highly skilled in the art of promoting learning. There is a huge amount that the Christian community can learn from secular education.[1] But the fact is that the Bible offers a different understanding of what it means to be human from a secular view. Education is the key mechanism whereby a society propagates its vision of being human. Clearly churches should have something to say about this.

A biblical paradigm

What does the Bible have to teach about our education system? How does it equip us to comment on issues such as vocational diplomas, teacher training, personalized learning and the nature and purpose of the curriculum when it was written in an age long before anyone had even the remotest glimmer of digital technology and climate change? 'Not directly,' is the answer. Our modern concept of state-funded schools, colleges and universities serving a religiously diverse democratic society was hardly in the mind of any of the biblical authors as they dipped their quills. We are unlikely to find texts that relate directly to the party manifestos. But it's a different matter when we come to the question of what education is for.

In his address to the 2007 General Assembly of the United Reformed Church, educationalist Professor Stephen Orchard[2] commented, 'We have not yet understood what is asked of us as disciples to make sense of a British society in which we are strangers.' Here Orchard advocates the biblical paradigm[3] of 'alien and stranger' (1 Peter 2.11) as a guiding principle for Christians. In the Petrine epistle, echoing Jesus' prayer for his disciples in John 17, the author reminds his readers that they have a special relationship with God as 'a chosen people, a royal priesthood, a holy nation, a people belonging to God' (2.9) which should shape their identity. In modern parlance, he is saying, 'Remember that, as a Christian, you have a distinctive worldview because of your relationship with Christ.'

This distinctive worldview has huge implications for education. At the heart of the Bible's teaching on learning is the concept of wisdom: the notion of sound judgements which arise out of right relationships with God and with our fellow humans. In other words, the framework or worldview within which we learn knowledge matters – hugely. Education is never neutral; it is always telling a story about what it means to be human. In the Bible we learn so as to know how better to love God and neighbour. An attachment to this distinctive worldview makes us strangers in the modern world of secularized education.

The themes of 1 Peter are reflected in the Old Testament story of Daniel.[4] At the beginning of a promising career Daniel was carried off to captivity in Babylon. Now he was an exile – an alien and stranger, weeping by the rivers of Babylon, wondering how he could possibly now sing the songs of the Lord (Psalm 137). The prospects for effective service in Jerusalem had been promising, but Babylon was an altogether different matter. Life looked pretty bleak.

But God had different ideas. Through the words of Jeremiah, he tells the beleaguered exiles that they are in the right place. Their job is to settle down, marry, work and, most importantly, 'seek the peace and prosperity of the city to which I have carried you into exile' (Jeremiah 29.7). They were to be faithful witnesses in Babylon. Daniel responded positively and became a transforming presence within the Babylonian system even though his Jewish faith made him an alien. Indeed, he became a trusted adviser to kings and was able to offer insights that drew on his Jewish worldview but that the Babylonians found compelling. He had learned to make sense of life, and be an influence in a society in which he was a stranger. Those seeking to bring a Christian voice to modern education face a similar challenge.

The current debate

What is there about education today that might mean Christians are aliens and strangers in their interaction with it? A comment made by Barry Sheerman MP, the Chairman of the Select Committee for the Department of Children, Schools and Families, will illustrate the issue. Talking about faith schools[5] he said, 'We all become a little more worried the more people take their faith seriously.'[6] The point he was making was echoed in the Runnymede Report on Church Schools[7] that seemed to argue that the ideal would be to have the ethos, culture and impact of faith schools without populating them with people of faith. Then everyone could benefit from them! In March 2009, the Liberal Democrats adopted similar policies. There seems to be a political aspiration to have the ethos and outcomes of faith schools available to the whole population, but without distinctive religious beliefs impinging.

Such attitudes derive from the widespread notion that religious faith is a matter of private quirks which should not have a shaping influence or presence in a public activity such as education. When I trained as a teacher in the 1970s this message was drummed into me. Things haven't much changed today. The expression of a distinctive Christian worldview creates unease in discussions of education.[8]

An interesting example is the recent debate about creationism.[9] An eminent science educator, Michael Reiss,[10] suggested that although creationism was not, in his view, a scientific theory, pupils' questions about it should be given serious attention if raised in science lessons. Subsequently the government published guidelines[11] in which it said that creationism was only to be discussed in Religious Education (RE) lessons. Such was the furore that Reiss was forced to resign his position as Education Officer at the Royal Society, apparently because talking about religious beliefs in science lessons violated science. It seems that matters to do with God have no place in science lessons, although it is apparently OK to talk about 'crazy' beliefs like creationism in RE.

This alien climate explains why some Christians have expressed considerable misgivings about the General Teaching Council's proposal to publish a new code of conduct requiring all teachers to promote equality and value diversity.[12] Will that be interpreted as meaning Christian teachers must keep silent about their faith? In the current climate it might.

The political debates about education will rage around issues like parent choice and power, the legitimacy or not of academies and faith schools, the promotion of human rights and community cohesion, university fees, academic standards, the National Curriculum and so forth. No doubt Christians will come to different conclusions as to the correct policies. But all of us should be pressing the politicians on the underlying message that their policies assume as to what it means to be human. Are students simply economic products of an educational machine or are we seeking to create people of wisdom? In the end is it only academic results that matter and, if not, how will their party rebalance the demands on schools to make other things really count? If we fail to speak *as Christians* on education will we have conceded too much to a secularist understanding of religion, namely that it is a problem that needs containing in the safe domain of people's private interests? As aliens and strangers, we need to demonstrate the public contribution that a distinctive Christian worldview makes.

A Christian response

To live like Daniel, as a stranger who becomes a transforming presence, requires us to become active, engaged participants in the system where God has placed us, able to discern how we offer a counter-cultural alternative to the way of thinking that dominates much modern education. The Christian faith offers a distinctive answer to the question, 'What is education for?'

There is, currently, an inherent contradiction in political aspirations. On the one hand, there is a huge emphasis on 'standards', 'excellence' and 'performance', which is closely linked to an economic agenda of raising national productivity. Schools are under huge pressure to generate ever better results from their pupils. This can distort their approach, as, for example, when a school spoke proudly of its stunning GCSE Science results gained by using a 70-slide PowerPoint presentation which students are shown three times in an hour before doing the end-of-module test the following week.[13] This is hardly education that will develop wisdom, although it seems to achieve the required exam results.

On the other hand, there is great emphasis on promoting pupils' well-being, which takes a much more holistic view of the child and is reflected in the most recent developments in the curriculum.[14] For example, the Every Child Matters (ECM) initiative[15] focuses on five areas of pupil development including staying safe and enjoyment and achievement. But each of these is subject to differing interpretation depending on your underlying worldview. Does, for example, 'staying safe' mean that safe sex will become the bedrock of sex education?

How does the 'stranger' paradigm help a Christian in commenting on such matters? There is clearly every reason to welcome the attention to pupil well-being. Less obvious perhaps, but I would also argue that a concern for high academic standards in education is 'to seek the welfare of the city'. But underpinning conceptions of both well-being and standards are views about what it means to be human. Here, there is definitely something *distinctive* for a Christian worldview to offer. Standards on their own become idols. Excellence should always be sought in servanthood, and not for selfish ends of personal advancement, wealth or status. Likewise, to take another example from the ECM programme, economic well-being should not mean just securing my own financial security. It should embrace a concern for others and, of increasing importance, for the environment. Christians can therefore actively embrace these political aspirations, but will seek to transform them by offering a distinctive view of what it means to be human. We will also want to integrate the 'standards' and 'well-being' agendas in ways that currently do not seem to be obvious to government. Personally, I doubt whether a Christian understanding of the pupil should ever allow schools to treat targets and results as ends in themselves.

Finally, the 'stranger' paradigm offers another significant perspective for Christians thinking about education. The call to be a stranger is not linked, contrary to what many assume, with a call to isolation, withdrawal and Christian protectionism. Rather, 1 Peter and Daniel challenge us to be involved with others in society in seeking the well-being of all. We may indeed be in sharp disagreement with our neighbours about many things, but our job is to 'seek the welfare of the city', not just to promote the interests of the Church. When we find ourselves in conflict with non-Christians, holiness is achieved in offering hospitality to our opponents.[16] Ultimately our goal should be that others will see our good works and glorify God (1 Peter 2.12).

Conclusion

In considering Christian engagement with education, the biblical paradigm of 'alien' and 'stranger' offers a model of how we should seek to exercise influence. Probably the most fundamental question that is thrown at Christians in current debates is, 'What right do you have to speak?' Many secular commentators interpret Christian involvement in education as fifth-column activity. Biblical strangers, however, are not like this. In offering a distinctive vision, they seek not power or preference but 'the welfare of the city'. They applaud the excellence that they find in education today, but offer an even better way through an alternative vision of what education is for. As strangers they practise hospitality to all around and seek to promote education that includes, honours and benefits the diverse citizens of modern Britain. But strangers are not deluded – they know they participate as aliens and that their alternative vision will sometimes attract assent and sometimes dissent.

When we meet the politicians at the hustings or on the doorsteps we of course will question them on their policies on parental choice, university fees, academic standards and much more. But if we are to fulfil our calling as aliens and strangers, we will also enquire as to their views on the underlying view of what it means to be human. Hopefully we can persuade them that wisdom is a goal worth striving for and make them a little more questioning about some of the assumptions that currently drive the system. And maybe they will also begin to value the distinctive Christian contribution a little more as a result of such encounters?

Notes

1 Spring Harvest in 2009 did this in taking learning as its theme.
2 Orchard directed the Christian Education Movement between 1986 and 2006.
3 See John Ashcroft, 'The Biblical Agenda: Issues of Interpretation', in *Jubilee Manifesto* (Nottingham: InterVarsity Press, 2005), for a discussion of biblical paradigm as an authority in shaping contemporary policy and practice. Tom Wright's well-known analogy of the unfinished Shakespeare play provides a similar model that we have utilized in the 'Transforming Lives' project to help Christian teachers reflect on the task of living under biblical authority in their professional work. See <www.transforminglives.org.uk/vocation.php>.
4 See Gerard Kelly, *Stretch: Lessons in Faith from the Life of Daniel* (Carlisle: Authentic, 2005), for detailed development of this theme.
5 Faith schools are those where the foundation means that religious faith is part of the defining ethos and culture of the schools.
6 In a Teachers TV programme *The Big Debate: Religion in Schools*. See <www.teachers.tv/video/24057>.
7 See <www.runnymedetrust.org/uploads/publications/Summaries/RightToDivide-Summary.pdf>.
8 For further discussion of the place of public theology, see publications from Theos <www.theosthinktank.co.uk>.
9 By creationism is meant literal belief in the process of creation described in Genesis.
10 Professor of Science Education, Institute of Education, University of London.
11 See <www.teachernet.gov.uk/docbank/index.cfm?id=11890>.
12 See *Times Educational Supplement*, 6 March 2009, p. 11.
13 As reported by Monkseaton High School, North Tyneside in the *Times Educational Supplement*, 30 January 2009. This smacks of a behaviourist approach which treats learning as little more than getting students to regurgitate correct answers. See <www.monkseaton.org.uk/Making_Minds/Pages/Spaced%20Learning%208%20minute%20lessons.aspx>.
14 The new National Curriculum puts much more emphasis on holistic learning and creativity and less emphasis on subjects and particular content.
15 See <www.everychildmatters.gov.uk>.
16 Luke Bretherton, *Hospitality as Holiness* (Farnham: Ashgate, 2006).

Further engaging

Publications

Jonathan Chaplin, *Talking God: The Legitimacy of Religious Public Reasoning* (London: Theos, 2008)

Margaret Cooling, *Creating a Learning Church* (Abingdon: Bible Reading Fellowship, 2005)

Trevor Cooling with Mark Greene, *Supporting Christians in Education* (London: Institute for Contemporary Christianity, 2008)

Terence Copley, *Indoctrination, Education and God: The Struggle for the Mind* (London: SPCK, 2005)

Grove Books Education Series (<www.grovebooks.co.uk>)

Jane Martin and Ann Holt, *Joined-up Governance* (Norwich: Adamson Publishing, 2002)

David Smith and John Shortt, *The Bible and the Task of Teaching* (Nottingham: The Stapleford Centre, 2002)

Nick Spencer, *Neither Private nor Privileged: The Role of Christianity in Britain Today* (London: Theos, 2008)

Websites

Association of Christian Teachers: <www.christian-teachers.org.uk>

Catholic Education Service: <www.cesew.org.uk>

Christian Schools Trust: <www.christianschoolstrust.co.uk>

Education Sunday: <www.educationsunday.org>

Festive: <www.festive.org.uk>. For those concerned with Further Education

Independent Schools Christian Alliance: <www.tisca.info>

National Society: <www.natsoc.org.uk>. Support for Anglican schools

The Stapleford Centre: <www.stapleford-centre.org>. For resources and training

Theos: <www.theosthinktank.co.uk>. A Christian voice in British politics

Transforming Lives: <www.transforminglives.org.uk>. See particularly the Toolkit for Churches

5

The Environment

HILARY MARLOW

Dr Hilary Marlow is a writer and researcher in environmental theology at the Faraday Institute for Science and Religion, where she is involved in a joint project with the Kirby Laing Foundation for Christian Ethics entitled 'Hope for Creation: A Biblical Vision for Contemporary Environmental Policy'. She is actively involved in the Christian environmental charities A Rocha and John Ray Initiative.

Introduction

Since the last election, concern about the environment has mushroomed. Even in the current economic downturn with its focus on recession and redundancies, renewable energy and recycling are matters for serious concern. So environmental issues are likely to play a significant part in the political rhetoric leading up to an election.

Although media attention is often focused on global climate change, this is just one of a number of interrelated issues that have significant implications for our planet. These include lack of clean drinking water, erosion and degradation of fertile agricultural land, increased risk of flooding as sea levels rise, irreversible destruction of wildlife habitats, increase in toxic waste and pollution.[1] The seriousness and complexity of these environmental issues mean it is crucial for Christians to be informed and to reflect on them in the light of biblical Christian faith.

Biblical perspectives

'Does the Bible really have anything to say about environmental issues?' you might ask. Certainly the biblical authors did not experience the same kind of damage to the planet that the industrialization and exponential population growth of the past couple of centuries have caused. Yet the Bible offers theological perspectives and ethical principles for living in a way that brings honour to God as well as respecting his world, which, as Chris Wright says, '[will] have a far-reaching impact on how biblically sensitive Christians will want to frame their ecological ethics today'.[2] Here then are some biblical principles which might guide our thinking.[3]

All creation reflects and celebrates God

We live in a world that is the creation of a loving God who has poured something of his own creativity into it and who values it all. The creation account of Genesis 1 repeatedly tells us, 'God saw that it was good' and the final verdict on the whole of his handiwork is that it is 'very good' (Genesis 1.31). The Bible reminds us that the creation reflects God's glory and majesty (e.g. Psalm 19.1–2). Its detailed descriptions of the natural world emphasize God's power as creator and sustainer; they also express a sense of wonder at the working of the natural world which reminds us of our transience (e.g. Psalm 104, Job 38—40). The psalmists call on the whole of the natural world, not just human beings, to give praise to the Lord (e.g. Psalm 150.6, 148.3–10). How we treat God's creation says something about our love and respect for the creator.

Our place in creation

The Genesis creation accounts provide two complementary understandings of our particular place within this wonderful creation. The first is that of exercising dominion over creation

(Genesis 1.28). This, coupled with the enigmatic statement that we are made 'in the image of God' (v. 27), is not a licence to exploit the rest of creation for our own ends.[4] Rather, it gives us, as creatures with highly developed moral awareness, a mandate from God to deal wisely and carefully with the rest of creation as his delegated representatives. It is to do with responsibilities, not rights. It involves the kind of servant leadership demonstrated by Christ, the ultimate 'image of the invisible God' (Colossians 1.15).

In Genesis 2 the Lord God forms the human being from the dust of the ground – a word play in Hebrew, *adam* from the *adamah* – and places him into the Garden of Eden to tend and protect it (v. 15). In Hebrew these words, so often translated 'to till and keep', can just as well be read as 'to serve and preserve' and remind us that we are servants of the one great king, God himself, with responsibility for tending his garden, the earth, as an act of service and worship towards him.

The link between human failure and environmental devastation

Just as the science of ecology describes the relationships between living species and their habitats, so too the Bible paints a clear picture of God's relationship with his creation, and especially of the fractured relationships within creation. A number of the Old Testament writers explicitly link environmental degradation and human moral and spiritual failure. In Hosea 4, the people forget God and his ways (v. 1), resulting in a breakdown in society (v. 2) accompanied by serious consequences for the natural world (v. 3, see also Isaiah 24.4–6; Jeremiah 12.11–12). Genesis 3 explains that one of the consequences of human disobedience is the struggle to make a living from the soil from which he was formed (vv. 17–19). The biblical story makes clear that human wrongdoing has a profound effect on the whole created order – and this is no less true today.

Hope for creation

Thankfully, this is not the end of the story, and both the Old and New Testaments offer the hope of reconciliation and renewal. This finds its ultimate expression in the incarnation, death and resurrection of Jesus Christ. The Lord of creation, who upholds its very existence, himself becomes part of his broken world in order to reconcile and complete it (Colossians 1:15–20). St Paul (Romans 8) speaks of the whole creation groaning as it waits for the revelation of God's children. He looks forward to the coming liberation of the whole creation as a result of the redemption of our human bodies. This involves restoration of the material world, including humanity, to all that God intended for it. Meanwhile we are to be participants in the reconciling work of Christ, as we pray 'your will be done, on earth . . .'

Pressing issues

In March 2009, climate scientists meeting in advance of the crucial UN climate change conference in December 2009 issued a grave warning about the failure of political leaders worldwide to face the scale and seriousness of environmental problems. In the UK, the current Labour government was instrumental in bringing climate change onto the agenda of G8 summits and has set apparently ambitious targets for the reduction of CO_2 emissions: but is it exercising the leadership necessary to bring about real practical change? Policy papers produced by the Conservative Party (*The Low Carbon Economy*) and the Liberal Democrats (*Zero Carbon Britain*) make impressive claims, but it would be naive to assume that behind the rhetoric there lies a realistic and attainable strategy.[5] Although the Green Party has an important and increasing voice in local politics, it is unlikely to become a major national political force in the foreseeable future. Since green issues, both global and national, will feature so prominently in the next election, here are some pressing questions to bring to the attention of our politicians.

What is your party's energy policy?

We live in an energy-dependent world, and it is estimated that three-quarters of our greenhouse gas emissions are due to energy use.[6] Coal is by far the dirtiest fossil fuel, and is still in abundant supply.[7] But we are rapidly using up world gas and oil reserves, which are estimated to reach peak production within the next 20 years.[8] Energy generation from renewable resources such as sun and wind is not yet able to provide more than a fraction of our needs. Nuclear energy is controversial but the best guarantee of future power needs, at least until renewable technology catches up. But nuclear energy is only available at present in developed countries – leaving China, for example, building new coal-fired power stations at the rate of two per week. A meaningful energy policy needs to consider not only the provision of 'clean' energy sufficient for domestic and industrial need, but also ways of reducing our power consumption and encouraging local, sustainable initiatives.

How will you reduce reliance on private vehicles?

At present rail travel prices make it often more expensive to go by train than to drive, and services are erratic and underfunded. To get people out of their cars, public transport needs to be efficient, reliable and, above all, affordable, and will require substantial government investment. In transport policies, as so many others, there is little evidence of 'joined-up' thinking. The current government's decision to go ahead with a third runway at Heathrow, in the face of considerable opposition, reflects their ambivalence over environmental matters – in the end, short-term economic gain is the driver.[9]

What is your party's view on wealth and sustainability?

At all levels our society remains driven by ever-increasing consumerism and materialism, although it doesn't seem that we are any happier than in the past.[10] This desire to acquire more and more is both unsustainable and unethical, yet the drive for continued economic growth is the foundation of most capitalist economies. For real change to come about, governments as well as individuals will need to think in terms of living sustainably, rather than increasing economic wealth. But is this something that our politicians are willing to face?

What about the global poor?

Environmental changes such as rising sea levels and soil degradation inevitably affect those who have the fewest resources, namely the world's poor. The effect of floods in low-lying areas such as Bangladesh is devastating for its inhabitants, many of whom live below the poverty line. Yet it is rich nations' use of fossil fuels that has helped create the climatic conditions which lead to such catastrophic flooding. It has been estimated that in 1995 there were about 25 million environmental refugees – people forced to migrate from their homeland because of environmental problems – and this figure is predicted to reach 200 million by 2050.[11] Where will they all go, and who will help them? Will they be welcomed in this country, or will it be a case of 'Not in my back yard'?

How do we provide for a growing world population?

The global population currently stands at almost 7 billion and is projected to grow to over 9 billion by the year 2050.[12] The resources of energy, water and food needed just to provide a basic standard of living for so many additional people will outstrip the current capacity of the earth to provide, assuming that we in the West want to retain our current standards of living. Should governments worldwide be encouraging their citizens to limit family size and provide the contraceptive resources to support this? And what right have we to deny the aspirations of those in developing countries who want the same levels of material prosperity, health care and education for their children that we now enjoy?

The long-term prospects: adaptation and mitigation?

At present political attention is focused on mitigating the effects of climate change by reductions in carbon emissions. But should governments also be devising measures to adapt to climate change and help ensure survival of humans and wildlife? And how far ahead should they be thinking – in terms of the next four-year election cycle or towards the well-being of our children and grandchildren?

Addressing these issues and others like them will not be easy. It will require courage, conviction and, above all, moral leadership on the part of our politicians. But it also requires the commitment of voters – people like you and me – to be a voice for change, to ask hard questions and to press for long-term, sustainable solutions.

Christian responses

In one sense, a Christian reaction to these issues may be no different from what any thoughtful, ethically minded person might decide. Yet the theological convictions outlined at the start offer a stronger, more coherent rationale for environmental concern than that provided by humanist or secularist thinking. Here are several ways in which Christians might want to respond to the challenges:

- On a personal level by deciding to adopt a simpler and more sustainable lifestyle, one that distinguishes between 'wants' and 'needs' and that tries to minimize our negative impact upon God's earth. This does not mean a list of dos and don'ts but is about discovering ways of living that honour him and respect his creation.[13] These changes can also be things we introduce into the communities of which we are part – neighbourhoods, workplaces, schools and churches.
- Politicians are very aware of public opinion, and particularly on a relatively high-profile issue such as the environment

they need to hear why it matters to us. Asking penetrating and informed questions of our MPs and local councillors forces them to do their homework and can help sharpen their focus. More than this, unless voters pressure politicians and give them 'permission' to pass tough legislation, it simply won't happen.

- Governments listen to the opinion of businesses and unions as well as individuals, and raising the profile of environmental issues in our workplace and staff associations can cause ripples in the political pond, as well as bringing about local change. So too can joining larger campaigns such as the Stop Climate Chaos coalition (<www.stopclimatechaos.org>).

- We are called to speak out on behalf of those who have no voice, just as biblical prophets like Amos and Micah were outspoken against Israel for its neglect of the poor. In today's global context, obeying the gospel injunction to 'love your neighbour as yourself' should include campaigning on behalf of a drought-ravaged community in sub-Saharan Africa, or a Bangladeshi farmer whose home and possessions and rice crop have been washed away by flood waters.

- In 2007 an Environment Agency survey of leading environmentalists and scientists asked them to name 50 things that will save the planet.[14] The role of faith communities and their leaders was listed second: 'It's time the world's faith groups reminded us we have a duty to restore and maintain the ecological balance of the planet.' What an encouragement for Christians to show that they are concerned and engaged with the issues of the twenty-first century. Whether this is demonstrated in practical, political or 'spiritual' activities, the Church has unique opportunities at a time of unique challenge.

The statistics and projections make grim reading; the solutions seem distant and elusive. Yet our Christian belief in a good God who created and sustains his world gives us a reason to work towards a sustainable future together.

Notes

1 For more details about the scope of the issues, see Martin J. Hodson and Margot R. Hodson, *Cherishing the Earth: How to Care for God's Creation* (Oxford: Monarch, 2008); James Gustave Speth, *The Bridge at the End of the World* (New Haven: Yale University Press, 2008), pp. 17–45.

2 Christopher, J. H. Wright, *Old Testament Ethics for the People of God* (Nottingham: InterVarsity Press, 2004), p. 144.

3 These are taken from Hilary Marlow, *The Earth Is the Lord's: A Biblical Response to Environmental Issues* (Cambridge: Grove Books, 2008).

4 As suggested in the highly influential article: Lynn White, Jr, 'The Historical Roots of Our Ecological Crisis' (*Science* 155, No. 3767, 1967), pp. 1203–7.

5 The policy papers can be downloaded from the respective party websites.

6 David McKay, *Sustainable Energy: Without the Hot Air* (Cambridge: UIT Cambridge, 2008), p. 16. This book can be downloaded free from <www.withouthotair.com>.

7 Nick Spencer and Robert S. White, *Christianity, Climate Change and Sustainable Living* (London: SPCK, 2007), p. 29.

8 According to the International Energy Agency, cited by George Monbiot, *The Guardian*, 18 December 2008, although exact predictions vary (see also McKay, *Sustainable Energy*, p. 5).

9 The *Stern Review* demonstrated that failure to tackle environmental issues would, in the end, have negative economic consequences. H. M. Treasury, *Stern Review on the Economics of Climate Change* (Cambridge: Cambridge University Press, 2006).

10 See discussion in Spencer, *Sustainable Living*, pp. 49–72; and Speth, *The Bridge*, pp. 129–34.

11 Norman Myers, 'Environmental Refugees: A Growing Phenomenon of the 21st Century' (*Philosophical Transactions*, B 357, No. 1420, 2002), pp. 609–13.

12 <http://www.un.org/apps/news/story.asp?NewsID=21847&Cr=populat&Cr1> (accessed 12 June 2009).

13 For suggestions on how to get started, see the A Rocha 'Living Lightly' website (<www.livinglightly24–1.org.uk>).

14 The Environment Agency, '50 Things That Will Save the Planet', *Your Environment Extra*, Vol. 17, Supp. 2007, <http://publications.environment-agency.gov.uk/pdf/GEHO0907BNFQ-e-e.pdf?lang=_e>

Further engaging

Publications

R. J. Berry (ed.), *When Enough is Enough: A Christian Framework for Environmental Sustainability* (Leicester: Apollos, 2007)

Dave Bookless, *Planetwise: Dare to Care for God's World* (Nottingham: InterVarsity Press, 2008)

Michael S. Northcott, *A Moral Climate: The Ethics of Global Warming* (Maryknoll, NY: Orbis Books, 2007)

Nick Spencer and Robert S. White, *Christianity, Climate Change and Sustainable Living* (London: SPCK, 2007)

Robert S. White (ed.), *Living Beyond Our Means: Christian Perspectives on Unsustainability* (London: SPCK, 2009)

Websites

A Rocha: <www.arocha.org>

Christian Ecology: <www.christian-ecology.org.uk>

Living Lightly 24-1: <www.livinglightly24–1.org.uk>

Eco-Congregation: <www.ecocongregation.org.uk>

The Jubilee Centre: <www.jubilee-centre.org/topics/the_environment>

Greenpeace: <http://www.greenpeace.org.uk/what-you-can-do/>

The Royal Society: <www.royalsociety.org>

The Intergovernmental Panel on Climate Change: <www.ipcc.ch>

6

International Order

BENEDICT ROGERS

Benedict Rogers is East Asia Team Leader at Christian Solidarity Worldwide, an international human rights organization. He authored *A Land Without Evil: Stopping the Genocide of Burma's Karen People*, and co-authored *On the Side of the Angels*. He also works as a freelance journalist, and human rights campaigner and fact finder. He has an MA in China Studies from the School of Oriental and African Studies, and wrote his dissertation on the Chinese Government's attitude towards Christianity. He regularly briefs British MPs, the European Union, UN officials, US Congressional offices and the State Department on human rights and religious freedom in Asia, and has testified in hearings at the European Parliament, the House of Commons, the US Congress and the Japanese Parliament. He is currently Deputy Chairman of the Conservative Party's Human Rights Commission.

'No man is an island, entire of itself . . . any man's death diminishes me, because I am involved in mankind', wrote John Donne four centuries ago. International events in recent years demonstrate clearly how true that principle is – that no person, and certainly no country, can live in isolation from others. Globalization, in all its forms, is here to stay.

The world has become increasingly interconnected and interdependent. The global financial crisis is the most recent example of this, but international terrorism, climate change, poverty, disease, trafficking of persons, drugs and arms, and the blatant disregard for human dignity and human life by tyrants and dictators in too many countries all illustrate the importance of international relations and foreign policy. Almost instant media reporting, combined with increased personal travel and communications through the internet, email, SMS text and other personal communication devices, ensure that those of us in the developed world, who have both resources and freedom, have no excuse for being unaware of what is happening on the other side of the world. The words of the Christian Parliamentarian William Wilberforce, speaking over 200 years ago when he introduced the bill to abolish the slave trade, have an even greater resonance to us today: 'We can no longer plead ignorance – we cannot turn aside.'

Profound challenges confront world leaders. The economic and political rise of China and India, the growing belligerence of Russia, the Israeli–Palestinian conflict, instability in Pakistan, Afghanistan, Iran, North Korea, nuclear proliferation, the rise of religious extremism and particularly radical Islamism and related terrorism, poverty and disease in Africa, trade justice and human trafficking, are just some of the issues which will face the next prime minister and foreign secretary of this country. The whole question of humanitarian intervention post-Iraq, the question of a 'just' war, the role of the United Nations, debates over the nature of sovereignty and the future shape of the European Union should be added to the list. The effectiveness of the UN's much trumpeted but so far unused 'Responsibility to Protect' mechanism, and questions relating to international justice for crimes against humanity, war crimes and genocide in light of the crises in Darfur, Zimbabwe and Burma, will also require attention. The continuing suppression of democracy, arbitrary arrest and torture of dissidents, religious persecution, denial of press freedom, the use of rape as a weapon of war, forced labour and the forcible conscription of child soldiers, bring issues of human rights to the fore. How much longer can the world allow dictators such as Robert Mugabe in Zimbabwe, Kim Jong-il in North Korea, Omar al-Bashir in Sudan or Senior General Than Shwe in Burma to oppress their people unchallenged?

Even in countries which are democratic, there remain major injustices. India, for example, has in many respects an impressive story to tell, as the world's largest multicultural, multi-religious democracy which has experienced extraordinary economic growth, remains shackled by the scandal of caste discrimination under which 250 million people are consigned to the dustbins of humanity, treated worse than animals. The rise of extremist Hindu nationalism, resulting in the violent persecution of Christians in significant parts of the country, is a related challenge. As a close friend with a shared history, Britain surely has a responsibility to help India overcome these twin plagues?

The words of Bob Dylan in his song 'Blowin' in the Wind' have a particular relevance to the challenges in the world today. He asks the following questions:

> How many years can a mountain exist
>   before it's washed to the sea?
> How many years can some people exist
>   before they're allowed to be free?
> How many times can a man turn his head,
>   pretending he just doesn't see?
> How many times must a man look up,
>   before he can see the sky?
> How many ears must one man have
>   before he can hear people cry?
> How many deaths will it take till he knows
>   that too many people have died?

These are surely the questions Christians should be asking today, for the Bible could not be clearer on the themes of freedom and justice. Throughout the Old and New Testaments there is a clear biblical mandate to speak up for justice, to work for freedom and to help the poor. In Isaiah 58.6–12 we are told that the 'type of fasting' we should choose is to 'loosen the chains of injustice' and 'set the oppressed free'. In Proverbs 31.8–9 it says: 'Speak up for those who cannot speak for themselves, for the rights of all who are destitute.' In Exodus, following the enslavement of the Israelites, God commanded Moses to go to Pharaoh and to say: 'Let my people go.' Is that not what Christians are called to do today, to go to the rulers of this world and say of the millions who are oppressed: 'Let my people go.'

The parable of the Good Samaritan is worth considering when reflecting on foreign policy. So many people around the world are like the man set upon by robbers, stripped, beaten and left half-dead – by dictators, war lords, terrorists, extremists, drug cartels and traffickers. The description in Psalm 10 applies to many situations in the world today. Describing the 'enemy', the psalmist writes: 'He lies in wait near the villages; from ambush he murders the innocent . . . He lies in wait to catch the helpless . . . His victims are crushed, they collapse, they fall under his strength'.

Is not the heart of Christianity a search for freedom, justice and peace? Jesus Christ knows about oppression, persecution and injustice. The world's most flagrant case of arbitrary arrest, its most prominent instance of religious persecution, its most brutal flogging, its most blatant travesty of justice, and the most infamous execution of an innocent man, were all endured by Jesus Christ. Should that not put his followers unequivocally on the side of the world's dissidents, refugees, political prisoners, persecuted religious minorities, slaves, child soldiers, and exploited, abused and raped women today?

In his book *Jesus of Nazareth*, Pope Benedict XVI writes:

> Knowing now from experience how brutally totalitarian regimes have trampled upon human beings and despised, enslaved and struck down the weak, we have also gained a new appreciation of those who hunger and thirst for righteousness: we have discovered the soul of those who mourn and their right to be comforted.[1]

Is there not therefore a biblical mandate for Christians to demand a foreign policy that helps the poor, liberates the oppressed and sets the captives free?

In 2007 we celebrated the bicentenary of the abolition of the transatlantic slave trade. We reflected on the example of William Wilberforce, supported by a coalition of activists who organized what was probably Britain's first public grassroots human rights campaign. The abolitionists used petitions, badges, public rallies, publications, letters to MPs and consumer boycotts. It is an inspiring example of what can be achieved through a combination of public pressure, parliamentary efforts and prayer. But as the Jubilee Centre's Cambridge Paper, *The Abolition of the Slave Trade: Christian Conscience and Political Action*, reminds us, 'the Christian campaigners were not naïve idealists and were not afraid to appeal to British interests'. There are lessons for our approach to foreign policy today.

A government is elected by the people of a country, to govern in the interests of that country. It is therefore absolutely correct that foreign policy should be shaped by national interest. However, in much of the debate about international relations, the issues are often presented as a choice between national interest and morality. This is wrong, and presents a false choice.

While there are sometimes tensions between short-term economic and strategic interests, and issues such as human rights, in the long term it is surely in our national interests to promote freedom and human rights, to address conflict, oppression and tyranny, and to fight poverty. History shows that in the long term, freedom is more conducive to prosperity and therefore to peace and stability. Dictators do not make reliable allies or business partners: they sow instability, reek of corruption, threaten their neighbours and, if left unchecked, threaten us. Many dictators are involved in the drugs trade, some have links with terrorism and have nuclear ambitions. Much of the world's poverty and many of the world's humanitarian crises are caused primarily by dictators. Furthermore, tyranny cannot last for ever. As the examples of South Africa, Indonesia and the countries of Eastern Europe show, oppressive regimes have been toppled – and sometimes replaced by former dissidents. If we have been allied to the oppressors, and have not helped those who struggle for freedom, then when they win their struggle they may be less likely to wish to befriend us. As Samantha Power argues in her book *A Problem from Hell*, 'Citizens victimised by genocide or abandoned by the international community do not make good neighbours, as their thirst for vengeance, their irredentism and their acceptance of violence as a means of generating change can turn them into future threats.' It is therefore in our own national interest to seek solutions to conflict, oppression and poverty.

At the heart of a Christian foreign-policy agenda should be the principles of freedom and justice for all. In addition to speaking up on behalf of fellow Christians who face persecution around the world, Christians who have the privilege of freedom should use their voice on behalf of others who are oppressed and persecuted as well: first because it is biblically and morally right to do so, second because it is in the interests of our nation, and third because it is in our own interests as Christians too. If Christians are seen to be more prominently campaigning for the oppressed and persecuted of other faiths, or of no faith, it is more likely that others, in turn, will speak out for the persecuted Church. If Christians were more active in, for example, the Free Tibet movement, or in speaking up for the Falun Gong in China or the Rohingya Muslims of Burma, would it not send a powerful message to the cynics and sceptics as well as to the oppressors and those who appease them? If Christians used their freedom to campaign more prominently for international action to address the gross human rights violations affecting all the people of Burma, Sudan, North Korea and Zimbabwe, regardless of religion, would that not win allies among other faiths and among the secular human rights groups who might then protest more actively than they have so far against the persecution of more than 200 million Christians in over 60 countries around the world? Christians have been at the forefront of trade justice and Make Poverty History campaigns. Is it not time to be on the front lines of international human rights advocacy? In *Justice, Mercy and Humility: Integral Mission and the Poor*, Gary Haugen, the founder of International Justice Mission, writes:

> The Spirit is inviting the church into a new era of advocacy that is as significant as the global missions movement of the past 150 years and the relief and development movement of the past 50 years. The need is no less great, nor the biblical mandate any less fundamental.

In addressing all the major international challenges outlined at the beginning of this essay, Christians should seek a consistent application of the values of freedom and justice, which ultimately will lead to peace. Poverty is caused largely by conflict, exploitation, oppression and injustice. It is therefore only by pursuing freedom and justice that we can even begin to address poverty, extremism and climate change, and only by staunchly defending freedom and justice that we can fight terrorism and international crime.

Politicians in all parties have made good statements on foreign policy. The former Labour Foreign Secretary Robin Cook pledged to pursue an 'ethical foreign policy'. In his speech to the Labour Party conference a month after 9/11, Tony Blair said: 'The starving, the wretched, the dispossessed, the ignorant, those living in want and squalor, from the deserts of northern Africa to the slums of Gaza, to the mountain ranges of Afghanistan – they too are our cause.' The Conservative Shadow Foreign Secretary William Hague has promised to 'put human rights at the very heart of foreign policy'. And David Cameron, to mark the sixtieth anniversary of the Universal Declaration of Human Rights, said:

> I want to say clearly to all those to whom freedom is denied, and whose basic rights are trampled upon: the Conservative Party stands with you and will speak up for you. Wherever we live, whatever our background, we share a common humanity. To people in Burma, in Russia, in Sudan, in North Korea – and indeed in Zimbabwe – whose rights are denied, I say that the Conservative Party will stand up for you in opposition and, if we are elected, in Government. We will always remember the appeal of Burma's opposition leader Aung San Suu Kyi: 'Please use your liberty to promote ours.' That is what we shall try to do, now and in the years ahead.

Christian voters of all political persuasions must hold the parties to such promises.

Note

1   Pope Benedict XVI, *Jesus of Nazareth* (Doubleday, 2007), p. 98.

Further engaging

Publications

Madeleine Albright, *The Mighty and The Almighty: Reflections on Faith, God, and World Affairs* (London: Pan Books, 2007)

Tony Carnes, 'Bush's Faith-Based Legacy' (*Christianity Today*, February 2009)

Tim Chester (ed.), *Justice, Mercy and Humility: Integral Mission and the Poor* (Carlisle: Authentic Media, 2002)

John Coffey, *The Abolition of the Slave Trade: Christian Conscience and Political Action* (Jubilee Centre Cambridge Papers, Vol. 15, No. 2, June 2006)

Joseph D'Souza and Benedict Rogers, *On the Side of the Angels: Justice, Human Rights and Kingdom Mission* (Carlisle: Authentic Books, 2007)

Michael Gerson, *Heroic Conservatism* (London: HarperCollins, 2007)

Os Guinness, *Unspeakable: Facing Up to Evil in an Age of Genocide and Terror* (London: HarperCollins, 2005)

Gary Haugen, *Good News About Injustice* (Nottingham: InterVarsity Press, 1999)

Benedict Rogers, *A Land Without Evil: Stopping the Genocide of Burma's Karen People* (Simpsonville, NC: Monarch, 2004)

Danny Smith, *Who Says You Can't Change the World?* (Spring Harvest, 2003)

Danny Smith, *Slavery Now and Then* (London: Kingsway, 2007)

John Stott, *New Issues Facing Christians Today* (Grand Rapids, MI: Zondervan, 1999)

Jim Wallis, *God's Politics* (London: HarperCollins, 2005)

Jim Wallis, *Seven Ways To Change the World* (Oxford: Lion Hudson, 2008)

Websites

Christian Solidarity Worldwide: <www.csw.org.uk>

Foreign and Commonwealth Office: <www.fco.gov.uk>

Freedom House: <www.freedomhouse.org>

Human Rights Watch: <www.hrw.org>

International Justice Mission: <www.ijm.org>

Micah Challenge: <www.micahchallenge.org>

7

Nationhood and Immigration

DEWI HUGHES with ROSE LYNAS

Dewi Hughes taught Religious Studies at the Polytechnic of Wales [now the University of Glamorgan] from 1975 to 1987. He then became Tearfund's first Co-ordinator for Wales and is currently Tearfund's Theological Adviser, and a member of The Lausanne Movement's Theology Working Group. He is author of *Meddiannu Tir Immanuel: Cymru a Mudiad Cenhadol y Ddeunawfed Ganrif*; *Has God Many Names? An Introduction to Religious Studies*; *God of the Poor: A Biblical Vision of God's Present Rule*; *Power and Poverty: Divine and Human Rule in a World of Need*; and *Castrating Culture: A Christian Perspective on Ethnic Identity from the Margins*.

Introduction

'British jobs for British workers', promised Gordon Brown at the annual Labour Party conference in September 2007. But who (not to mention, what) did he mean? Did his definition of 'British' include the 6.5 million people born overseas who were resident in the UK in the year to June 2008, or the 25,670 people who applied for asylum in 2008?

What does it mean to be British, when the United Kingdom has such a diverse and colourful ancestry – from the indigenous Britons (whoever they were) to the invading Romans, Angles, Saxons, Danes, Normans and others, to the Afro-Caribbean, Asian and Eastern European immigrants of recent years? Concentrations of English people in Wales (as well as Scotland and Ireland, and vice versa), often with their own language and/or identity, raise similar questions. Interestingly, so-called 'ethnic minorities' often have a stronger British identity than 'native' whites. The 2001 General Household Survey found that 51 per cent of minority ethnic groups describe themselves only as British, compared with 29 per cent of whites. By contrast, 70 per cent of whites describe themselves as primarily belonging to one of the United Kingdom's four constituent nations, compared with just 14 per cent of minority ethnic groups.[1]

Politicians refer to 'this nation', and Christians pray for 'our nation', both meaning Britain – despite the fact that many Scottish, Irish, Welsh and English people consider these countries their respective nations. Politicians often appeal to 'Britishness' as a value, and our national identity is a theme that provokes strong reactions.

The concept of nationhood is inextricably entwined with our approach to immigration. The ambiguous nature of 'Britishness' means that immigration is subject to misunderstanding, propaganda and statistical manipulation. Half-truths abound – one reason that the British National Party (BNP) has been able to make such gains in recent years. One of the misconceptions involves the scale of immigration. A 2007 MORI poll showed that '*Daily Express* readers believed that 21 per cent of the population were immigrants, *Daily Mail* readers thought that 19 per cent of the population were immigrants, and *Guardian* readers thought that 11 per cent of the population were immigrants. In reality 7 per cent of the population were immigrants.'[2] Our national identity and its implications for immigration is a subject that requires clarity of thought.

The biblical picture

A biblical understanding of nationhood is fundamental for a Christian idea of Britishness. This will provide a framework within which immigration can also be viewed.

According to Genesis 10, the development of nations was a natural consequence of the expansion of humankind over the earth as God intended (Genesis 1.28a). As people multiplied and spread, different languages developed, and those speaking the same language, when concentrated in a territory, became known as distinct nations (Genesis 10.5, 20, 31–2). The nations of Genesis 10 were groups of people who shared a name that was often that of a common ancestor, and who came to share a history and a culture that included customs, language and territory.

Interestingly, five of the six recognized characteristics of ethnic groups in contemporary anthropological theory are in evidence in the table of nations in Genesis 10. They are:

1   a common proper name;
2   a myth of common ancestry;
3   memories of a common past;
4   elements of a common culture, which normally includes religion, custom or language; and
5   a link with a homeland.

The only one missing is a sense of solidarity, but that can almost be assumed to be present if the other five characteristics are present.[3] In Genesis, what anthropology calls 'ethnic groups' are called 'nations'.

The story of the Tower of Babel (Genesis 11.1–9) follows the description of the development of nations. This story highlights the sinful human propensity to thwart the formation of nations as God intended, identifying themselves by geographic location and boasting in their own achievements rather than as created beings subject to God. In thwarting Babel's inward-looking self-definition by confusing its language, God was enabling the fulfilment of his creation mandate to fill the earth (Genesis 1.28), facilitating the process of the development of nations as he had intended, as described in Genesis 10. One warning – though not one explicitly stated – is that this kind of arrogance can result in nationalism and imperialism. In the biblical account of nationhood there is no room for idolatrous loyalty to the nation – as happens in later Babylonian ideological nationalism.[4]

The Table of Nations and the Tower of Babel present us with a vivid picture of how nations are formed and destroyed in a fallen world. Deuteronomy 2.9–12, 19–23 contains what, on first sight, seem like obscure notes, which the NIV puts in parentheses, about the movements of nations in the area East of the Jordan. But these verses declare unambiguously that ultimately God directs the destiny of nations according to his sovereign purposes.[5] Paul affirms this Old Testament conviction in his sermon to the Athenian intellectuals: 'From one man [God] made every nation of men, that they should inhabit the whole earth; and he determined the times set for them and the exact places where they should live.'[6]

In contrast to the human propensity to build empires and subjugate other nations, is God's redemptive purpose from Israel's beginning with Abraham to be a means of blessing to all the nations (Genesis 12.3, 18.18, 22.18). This is nowhere clearer than in Isaiah and his vision of the glorious consummation of history when all the nations will bring their offerings to mount Zion (Isaiah 60.3ff, 66.18; cf. Zechariah 8.23). This theme is taken up again in Revelation when John sees the nations walking in the light of the eternal kingdom of the Lamb and the leaves of the trees on each side of the river of life bringing healing to the nations from the curse of war (Revelation 21.24, 22.1–3a).

Intertwined with the biblical concept of nationhood is that of the 'resident alien'; both nationhood and 'immigration' were deeply embedded in Israel's national identity. Israel's first Patriarch, Abraham, was called by God to leave Ur to settle in Canaan. His descendants later settled in Egypt due to a famine in Canaan. The Israelites were reminded of this fact when they gave their firstfruits and tithes to the Lord, when they declared: 'My father was a wandering Aramean, and he went down to Egypt with a few people . . .' (Deuteronomy 26.5). The Israelites' captivity under Pharaoh, culminating in the Exodus, were continual reminders of the need to treat other aliens well. 'Do not oppress an alien; you yourselves know how it feels to be aliens, because you were aliens in Egypt' (Exodus 23.9).

Within Israel, immigrants were broadly divided into two categories: the *gēr* and the *nokrî*.[7] *Gērîm* (plural of *gēr*) were those who

– though foreign born – lived alongside the Israelites as fellow countrymen. Immigration involved at least a measure of assimilation into their new culture – though they were still recognized as *gēr*, so ethnic identity was not considered irrelevant. They were subject to the same rules, responsibilities and privileges (Leviticus 19.33–34). For example, they were not to work on the Sabbath, and their employers were not to force them to do so. Interestingly, in the Greek Septuagint translation of the Old Testament, *gēr* is always translated *proselytos* (proselyte, convert). This confirms the presumption of assimilation or integration and explains the inclusive legislation concerning the *gērîm*. They are often mentioned in a context of poverty or economic dependence, alongside the orphan and widow, suggesting that they were frequently among the most vulnerable of society. They were not to be ill-treated (Exodus 22.21–22; Leviticus 19.33; Psalm 146.9; Zechariah 7.10); they were to be loved (Leviticus 19.34); they were to be included (Leviticus 19.10, 23.22; Deuteronomy 16.11, 14, 24.19–21). The overlap with many modern-day refugees and asylum-seekers to the UK is obvious, as is the principle that the needy should not be exploited, foreign-born or otherwise.

The other major category of immigrants were the *nokrîm*. These immigrants strongly retained their own national identity; their integration and consequently their rights in Israel's culture were far more limited. For example, the only people the ban on charging interest did not apply to within Israel were the *nokrîm* (Deuteronomy 23.19–20). This may seem unfair, as demanding interest is generally seen in terms of injustice in the Old Testament. However, if a *nokrî* was charged interest but in turn charged it in his own dealings (according to his own custom) he would be at an unfair advantage. It was also the case that the *nokrîm* could subvert their host culture by leading the Israelites astray – most famously in the case of Solomon's foreign wives, who abetted his idolatry, and Ahab's Sidonian wife Jezebel. In the case of Naboth's vineyard, Jezebel was able to insinuate a way of exercising power into Israel that was totally opposed to what God had revealed to the Israelites.[8]

The United Kingdom in the twenty-first century is very different from ancient Israel, but there are principles in the Old Testament teaching on 'immigrants' that are still applicable. Immigrants who respect our culture should be welcomed, but we should be wary of those who seek to subvert it.

Unity in diversity is the key principle in New Testament teaching on ethnic identity. This means both the positive affirmation of unity across ethnic lines and the affirmation of ethnic difference. When Paul says that 'there is neither Jew nor Greek . . . for you are all one in Christ Jesus' (Galatians 3.28), he is not saying that Jews cease to be Jews and Greeks cease to be Greeks when they become Christian. What he is saying is that all detrimental distinctions between Jews and Greeks are dissolved in Christ. Faith in Christ means the death of self-aggrandizing nationalism. At the foot of the cross as people who are Jewish, Greek, English, Welsh, Scots, Pakistani, Afro-Caribbean, etc., we together realize that God 'chose the lowly things of this world and the despised things . . . so that no one may boast before him' (1 Corinthians 1.28–29). We still rejoice in what we are as a manifestation of God's good providence, but we no longer feel that rejoicing in our own identity means that we must rubbish the identity of others.

A Christian response

What does the biblical teaching mean for the concept of nationhood? God's redemptive purpose is to bless the nations, although ultimately God's blessing of a nation is linked to its welcoming of Jesus as the Messiah. The biblical picture suggests that we need to look at the issues of national identity and immigration from the perspective of the alien – whether modern-day '*gēr*' or '*nokrî*' – as much as from our own. As well as countering the misleading and sometimes unpleasant spin and exaggeration, we need to consider the Bible's moral imperative to love the alien. The implied economic warning about the *nokrî* in Deuteronomy 23 raises the question of how best to deal with those who intend to exploit the system; however, although immigration should ideally be a two-way process and privileges should go hand in hand with responsibilities, the overwhelming biblical emphasis on compassion and justice should lead to caution when it comes to knee-jerk reactions.

One problem concerns the language we use, with words for distinct categories popularly considered as freely interchangeable. The general term 'immigrant' has no clear definition, but is usually accepted to mean one who has settled as a long-term resident in another country.[9] 'Asylum-seekers' are those who have fled their country of origin and applied for asylum in another country; these are regularly lumped together with 'refugees', who live outside of their country of origin due to fear of persecution. All of these are frequently confused with 'illegal immigrants' – those who live outside their country of origin without the legal permission of their country of residence. Another term that has increasingly been used recently is 'migrant worker' or 'economic migrant' – those who come to the country to find paid employment, either on a short- or long-term basis. Obviously these categories overlap and include a wide range of people and reasons for immigration. We must be conscious of, and cautious with, the language we use to avoid misrepresentation, and similarly hold our politicians to account.

Gordon Brown's promise of 'British jobs for British workers' sits slightly uneasily against his insistence to the G20 that protectionism is not a wise response to the global recession,[10] and could risk repeating the mistakes of the Great Depression. The government is in the process of passing its seventh immigration bill in ten years. In the white paper 'Making Change Stick' the government sets out its aims to simplify the system, strengthen borders and introduce a points-based system for newcomers. A key aim is 'ensuring newcomers earn the right to stay by learning English, paying taxes and obeying the law' (p. 1). Do these changes respect the principles relating to the *gērîm* and *nokrî*?

The complexity, fluidity and long-term nature of nationhood and immigration issues mean that one or other party's policies cannot easily or immediately be judged on their success. Instead, it is the overall vision of Britain, and its implications for 'British-ness', that can guide us. Is 'British' an inclusive or exclusive label – a way we welcome and integrate others, or separate ourselves and keep others out? The moral imperatives of the Bible are to treat the resident alien compassionately, and not to lose sight of our loyalty to God – or our humanity – in our pursuit of nation-hood. From a biblical perspective it is the respect of difference and the warmth of the welcome that are most likely to lead to a place of peace that will leave no one unchanged.

Notes

1 <www.statistics.gov.uk/lib2001/Section3658.html> (accessed 8 May 2009).
2 <www.guardian.co.uk/media/2007/jan/23/pressandpublishing. immigrationasylumandrefugees> (accessed 14 April 2009).
3 John Hutchinson and Anthony D. Smith (eds), *Ethnicity* (Oxford: Oxford University Press, 1996), pp. 6–7.
4 To complete the picture here we would need to consider the complex and profound biblical concept of the moral purpose of God in his direction of the nations. For a brief and inadequate discussion of this, see Dewi Hughes, *Castrating Culture: A Christian Perspective on Ethnic Identity from the Margins* (Carlisle: Paternoster, 2001), pp. 71–3.
5 For a fine exposition of these verses see Christopher Wright, *New International Biblical Commentary, Deuteronomy* (Carlisle: Paternoster, 1996), p. 36.
6 Acts 17.26. Some other passages that make the same point are Deuteronomy 26.19; Job 12.23; Psalm 22.27–8, 47.8, 86.9; Daniel 12.1.
7 See Jonathan Burnside, *Status and Welfare of Immigrants*, especially pp. 10–21.
8 See Dewi Hughes, *Power and Poverty: Divine and Human Rule in a World of Need* (Nottingham: InterVarsity Press, 2008), pp. 72–3.
9 See *Votewise* (1st edn), p. 21.
10 <http://news.bbc.co.uk/1/hi/business/7728929.stm> (accessed 14 April 2009).

Further engaging

Publications

Jonathan P. Burnside, *The Status and Welfare of Immigrants: The Place of the Foreigner in Biblical Law and its Relevance to Contemporary Society* (Cambridge: Jubilee Centre, 2000)

Dewi Hughes, *Castrating Culture: A Christian Perspective on Ethnic Identity from the Margins* (Carlisle: Paternoster Press, 2001)

R. Tudur Jones, *The Desire of Nations* (Llandybie: Christopher Davies, 1974)

Will Kymlicka, *Politics in the Vernacular: Nationalism, Multiculturalism, and Citizenship* (Oxford: Oxford University Press, 2001)

Fearghas MacFhionnlaigh, 'Creative Tensions: Personal Reflections of an Evangelical Christian and Gaelic Poet', *Scottish Bulletin of Evangelical Theology*, Vol. 14, No. 1, 1996, pp. 37–50

Nick Spencer, *Asylum and Immigration: A Christian Perspective on a Polarised Debate* (Milton Keynes: Paternoster Press, 2004)

William F. Storrar, '"Vertigo" or "Imago"? Nations in the Divine Economy', *Themelios*, Vol. 21, No. 3, April 1996, pp. 4–9

Miroslav Volf, *Exclusion and Embrace: A Theological Exploration of Identity, Otherness and Reconciliation* (Nashville: Abingdon Press, 1996)

8

Tax and Benefits

JO HOLLAND

Jo Holland works as Senior Researcher to Steve Webb MP and runs his
Parliamentary office in Westminster. She has nearly ten years' experience
contributing to policy development within the Liberal Democrats,
specializing in benefits and pensions, and issues relating to children and the
family. She has co-authored two book chapters and acted as a research
associate for the Relationships Foundation on tax and benefits issues. She
has a first-class degree in History from Cambridge University, and is an
executive member of the Liberal Democrat Christian Forum.

Introduction

We are all affected by the way in which governments choose to
collect and spend our money. All of us pay taxes (from VAT to
petrol duties to income tax) and have an interest in how they are
spent, whether on 'public goods' such as schools, roads and
defence, or on welfare provision. And at some stage in our lives,
the majority of us will come into contact with at least one of the
benefits offering financial support to families with children, the
unemployed, sick and disabled people, and the elderly.

A nation's tax and benefits system reflects its government's
beliefs about wealth redistribution and the organization of economic activity. This chapter seeks to make sense of the issues and
to set out some principles to assist Christians wanting to engage
with today's political debate.

A biblical paradigm

We cannot simply transplant the rules governing an ancient society into our own, but we can apply underlying biblical principles to think about how our society collects taxes and distributes benefits:

God gives generously to us and we should give generously back to him

In the days before Israel's kingship, the people were expected to give back one-tenth of their produce to God, their ultimate ruler: 'A tithe of everything from the land, whether grain from the soil or fruit from the trees, belongs to the Lord' (Leviticus 27.30). This suggests that our wealth is not ours to do with exactly as we wish.

God requires us to give back to those who have less

Tithing was separate from the freewill offerings that people were also expected to give. It was therefore a tax, and a proportion of that collected was distributed to the poor, as welfare. The people brought their tithes into the towns so that the 'aliens, the fatherless and the widows . . . [could] come and eat and be satisfied', at which the Lord would bless the people 'in all the work of [their] hands' (Deuteronomy 14.28–29). When asked whether the Jews should pay taxes to their occupying Roman rulers, Jesus said, 'Give to Caesar what is Caesar's, and to God what is God's' (Matthew 22.21). In our political system, we elect our government and give it a mandate to collect taxes from us to spend on our behalf, while recognizing that the Lord is still our ultimate ruler.

God expects us to care for one another

Throughout the Books of the Law, provision is made for the poor and unfortunate. The principle of Jubilee required the restoration of lands to their original owners every 50 years, to ensure that the Israelites did 'not take advantage of each other' (Leviticus 25.17). Debts were to be cancelled after seven years (Deuteronomy 15). Families were expected to care for one another, and the kinsman-redeemer would intervene if a poor relation was obliged to sell his property or to sell himself into slavery (Leviticus 25). Farmers were to leave gleanings[1] for the poor to gather after the harvest, as we see in the story of Ruth and her kinsman-redeemer Boaz.

Neighbours were to help each other in times of trouble and 'if there is a poor man among your brothers in any of the towns of the land that the Lord your God is giving you . . . be open-handed and freely lend him whatever he needs' (Deuteronomy 15.7–8). It is clear that, just as God was generous in giving the land to the people, so he expects his people to be generous to one another.

We also have a responsibility to look after ourselves

We should not assume that anyone else owes us a living. Paul warns against idleness and emphasizes that he worked hard for his living so that he did not become an unnecessary burden on his friends. He warns that: 'If a man will not work, he shall not eat' (2 Thessalonians 3.6–10). We have a responsibility to earn our living as far as we can.

God is compassionate towards the needy

Jesus spent his time mainly with the poor and the outcast, not the wealthy and important, and provided food for the hungry crowds (Matthew 14.13–21, 15.29–38). God empties himself and personally reaches down and 'raises the poor from the dust and lifts the needy from the ash heap' (Psalm 113.7). And he expects his people to do the same, praising rulers who 'deliver the needy who cry out, the afflicted who have no-one to help' (Psalm 72.12).

We are commanded to follow God's example: to give back from what we have been given, to be open-handed towards the poor, but also to take responsibility for making a living for ourselves when we can. How do we see these principles played out in the complex twenty-first-century relationship between citizen and state?

The current debate

In modern British politics our view of the role of the tax and benefits system hinges on our view of the role of the state, and how much it should intervene in people's lives.

The taxation debate centres on three main issues. First, how much tax should the government collect altogether? Second, what kinds of goods should be taxed, and should taxation be used to influence behaviours? Depending on the outcome that parties are trying to achieve they may place different emphases on the taxation of, for example, individuals, savers, businesses, inheritance, petrol, alcohol and pollution. Third, how should taxation be structured between groups within society? Taxation might be progressive (where those earning more pay a larger percentage of their income in tax) or regressive (each person pays the same amount of money in tax regardless of their income).

A reduction in certain taxes, such as income tax, where the wealthier pay a higher rate, might be compensated for by an increase in taxes such as council tax, VAT or alcohol duty, which tend to be paid disproportionately by the least wealthy (£1 a week council tax increase will have a proportionately larger impact on lower earners).

The Conservatives have traditionally supported light taxation, broadly believing that people work hard to earn their money, and that high taxes discourage economic activity. A low-tax economy with minimal state intervention makes everyone more prosperous and the poor become wealthier as a result. Labour has historically favoured a more interventionist position, where the state uses the tax and benefits system to shift wealth from the richer to the poorer. Left to themselves, markets create uneven outcomes and so the state acts as supplier and enabler, often contracting out services to private and voluntary providers. The Liberal Democrats tend slightly more towards the latter view, but believe that the state works best when it is as local, flexible and accountable as possible.

Turning to welfare, recent reforms have been guided by Labour's belief that work is the best route out of poverty and gives people a sense of self-worth. It has pledged to abolish child poverty by 2020. Through the concept of conditionality, people must increasingly carry out voluntary work, or some activity preparing them for work, in return for their benefits. The Conservatives also favour work to lift people out of welfare, and view benefit dependency as a major cause of low aspiration and social breakdown. The Liberal Democrats believe it is wrong to coerce vulnerable groups into working for their benefits, and call on the state to 'lend a helping hand' to those in need.[2]

As an idea of the scale of the issues, the total tax and National Insurance contributions flowing into the Treasury are worth £500 billion a year.[3] The Department for Work and Pensions, which administers the benefits system, has an annual expenditure of almost £150 billion.[4] What does this £150 billion pay for? At the time of writing[5] there are about 12 million pensioners, 3.2 million families with a disabled member, 5.7 million carers,[6] 6 million families claiming child tax credits,[7] and nearly 4 million households claiming housing benefit to help pay their rent. There are 2 million unemployed people, a number that is likely to rise as recession deepens. And despite all the available tax credits and benefits, there are still 13 million people at the start of the twenty-first century who live below the government's official 'poverty line'.[8]

Does this mean that benefit levels are too low? Or does it mean that government should pay more attention to causes, such as why someone is poor in the first place? One causal factor is personal debt which, in the form of credit cards, loans, mortgages and overdrafts, has increased to more than a trillion pounds (i.e.

double the government's entire annual tax take), as people have borrowed money in prosperous times to fund lifestyles beyond their means. Now that the boom is over, the main thrust of political debate is about how to pull the UK back from recession.

As the election approaches, the parties will be putting forward their proposals to tackle these deep-seated issues, and each of us must decide how to vote.

A Christian response

People cast their vote for all kinds of reasons. We must accept that no party has any magic-bullet solutions, and we should vote according to how we believe they approach the issues. Here are a few principles to guide our thinking.

Do we see in parties' tax and benefits proposals a sense of compassion towards the poor and the marginalized?

1 John 3.17 says: 'If anyone has material possessions and sees his brother in need but has no pity on him, how can the love of God be in him?' What are the parties' approaches towards the very elderly, carers, people who are long-term sick or disabled, those who fall between all the means of self-support? These people tend to be poorer. Are they recognized in spending priorities, grudgingly or generously?

Do we see a relational approach to policy?

The individual is not a stand-alone being. We are part of families and communities, with a responsibility to look out for one another. The second greatest commandment is, 'Love your neighbour as yourself.' Jesus also said, 'Where your treasure is, there will your heart will be also' (Matthew 6.21). Obviously it is hard for a government in a country of 60 million people to treat everyone as a human being rather than a statistic, but we can get an idea of some of their priorities from their spending choices.

In the party manifestos, are people rewarded more for 'living to work' or for 'working to live'? Is parenthood seen as worthwhile in itself, or as a distraction from encouraging women back into paid work? Are carers of the sick, disabled and elderly valued for what they do? Are people viewed as human beings with an inherent worth? Are people encouraged to take responsibility for their own lives?

Another question to consider is whether the tax and benefits system should be designed to incentivize certain behaviours, such as marriage, or whether it should focus on alleviating poverty in the poorest households, regardless of their make-up. We can look at whether policies are designed to 'support' families; whether they enable families to stay together, to spend time together, to build stable family forms and strong relationships.[9] However, we must also look at what kind of help is offered to those who have already experienced family breakdown. It may be good to support marriage, but it does not mean that single parents should be neglected. They are often poorer financially than couples, and generally do not choose to be single, with the burden of struggling to raise a child alone.

Do policies look at the causes of problems as well as the consequences?

If an ambulance is called to treat people who have fallen off a cliff, not only will the medics treat the wounded at the bottom, but someone should also go to the top to stop people falling off in the first place.

Financial hardship may be seen to generate problems such as stress and depression, lack of time to build relationships, and anxiety about money. Factors that can be traced back to poverty – as both causes and consequences – include poor housing conditions, poor educational achievement, lack of aspiration among young people, unemployment, poor mental health, and a feeling of alienation from society.

This debate ranges far wider than a simple discussion of the optimal levels of taxes and benefits, and it is important to look at whether the party manifestos recognize and address these issues.

This is by no means an exhaustive list of principles but will perhaps help us to think biblically about how we cast our vote.

Conclusion

Finally, it is important to remember that Christians are to be found in all the main political parties, and that none of the parties claim to reflect a Christian worldview to the electorate. Therefore it is inevitable that Christians wanting to engage with the political system must look at their own priorities in the light of their faith, while recognizing that no party will get it right all the time.

Notes

1   The remainders from the harvesting of grain, cf. Ruth 2.
2   Freedom from Poverty, Opportunity for All, Policy Paper 80, Liberal Democrats, 2007, pp. 4–5, at: <www.libdems.org.uk/media/documents/policies/80-FreedomFromPoverty.pdf>.
3   2008 Pre-Budget Report, HM Treasury, November 2008, Annex B, table B12, at: <www.hm-treasury.gov.uk/prebud_pbr08_repindex.htm>. This includes income tax and National Insurance contributions along with other taxes, including VAT, capital gains tax, corporation tax, inheritance tax, stamp duties, alcohol and tobacco duties, vehicle excise duties, council tax and business rates.
4   Total departmental spending by 2010–11 is projected to be £149,378 million: Departmental Report 2008, Department for Work and Pensions, p. 98, table 1, at: <www.dwp.gov.uk/publications/dwp/2008/dr08/Fullreport.pdf>.
5   Spring 2009.

6   E. Holzhausen and V. Pearlmann, *Caring on the Breadline* (Carers National Association, now Carers UK, 2000).

7   Although these are virtually universal benefits as they are available to people with fairly high incomes. They also come out of the Treasury's budget, not the Department for Work and Pensions'.

8   Households Below Average Income statistics 2006/07, Department for Work and Pensions, table 3.3, p. 56, at: <www.dwp.gov.uk/asd/hbai/ hbai2007/pdf_files/full_hbai08.pdf>. Calculated as the number of individuals with incomes below 60 per cent median income after housing costs have been taken into account.

9   Definitions from Relationships Foundation: <www.relationshipsfoundation.org>.

Further engaging

Publications

Conservative policy paper, 'Reconstruction: Plans for a Strong Economy, 2008

Conservative policy paper, 'Work for Welfare', January 2008

Labour's Welfare Reform White Paper of December 2008, 'Raising Expectations and Increasing Support: Reforming Welfare for the Future'

Liberal Democrat policy paper, 'Freedom from Poverty, Opportunity for All', Autumn 2007

Liberal Democrat policy paper, 'Reducing the Burden', Autumn 2007

Poverty and Justice Bible, Bible Society, <www.povertyandjusticebible.org>

John R. W. Stott, *New Issues Facing Christians Today* (Basingstoke: Marshall Pickering, 1999)

Christopher Townsend, 'Render unto Caesar? The Dilemmas of Taxation Policy', *Cambridge Papers*, September 2001, <www.jubilee-centre.org>

9

Employment

MARTIN CLARK

Martin Clark is Development Director of Citylife, Cambridge, a social enterprise spun out of the Relationships Foundation in 1999 to tackle urban unemployment through charitable bonds – an innovative form of financial products to support enterprise, employment and social inclusion projects. He is the author of *The Social Entrepreneur Revolution* (Marshall Cavendish Business, January 2009).

Employment

It remains a modern paradox that while some always have too much paid work, others have little or none. In a recession, and planning for recovery, this becomes more critical. How do we ensure access to jobs for as many as want them? How do we balance work and life? Can our experience of employment be made more positive and purposeful? Biblical thinking offers much to this debate, and to Christians seeking to engage with it.

I focus on paid employment (though using the terms 'work' and 'jobs' interchangeably where the meaning is clear), unemployment, recent policy changes, and the political debate about future priorities.

A biblical paradigm

When considering work, Christians should recall that Jesus began his employment in his earthly father's carpentry workshop – the family business – and undertook his heavenly Father's work of redemption and salvation of the human race (John 5.36). Work is central to the biblical narrative because we are made in the image of a God who works creatively and, in resting, instituted the Sabbath. Craftspeople work to serve God in building the Temple (Exodus 31, 36). Working people abandon jobs to follow Christ. Paul worked in support of the gospel by tent-making (Acts 18.3) and commanded the Corinthians to 'work hard with your own hands' (1 Corinthians 4.12). For others, work impedes discipleship, illustrating the dangers of over-attachment to work or its rewards.

Jesus shows familiarity with the suffering of landless casual labourers in the parable of the workers in the vineyard (Matthew 20.1–16). The story's twist sees the kingdom of God unexpectedly thrown open to latecomers (Gentiles) and characterized by an other-worldly excess of generosity by the employer. None can escape Jesus' piercingly simple injunction, underscored by Paul and still used today, that 'workers deserve their wages' (Luke 10.7; 1 Timothy 5.18) – itself linked to the Old Testament command not to withhold wages of a hired worker overnight because 'he may cry to the Lord against you, and you will be guilty of sin' (Deuteronomy 24.15). The fruits of work are for worship and providing for the poor, widow and alien – for example through leaving unharvested margins for gleaning (Leviticus 19.9–10). Work should help the poor and not be exploitative: 'If one of your countrymen becomes poor among you . . . help him as you would an alien or temporary resident . . . do not make him work as a slave. He is to be treated as a hired worker . . . he is to work for you until the Year of Jubilee' (Leviticus 25.35–42).

The Jubilee principle was to ensure periodic redistribution of land and cancellation of debts, rebalancing society to avoid extremes of wealth or poverty. Implementing the injunction to offer work to whoever falls into poverty (without judging whether they are 'deserving') means 'there should be no poor among you' (Deuteronomy 15.4). In the Bible's pastoral and agricultural societies, access to land governed families' means to livelihood; for most in the twenty-first century our livelihood derives from employment. So biblical principles covering the means to livelihood remain relevant today. Above all, the refrain 'do not take advantage of one another' (e.g. Leviticus 25.17) encompasses all economic relationships, setting a clear moral framework for contracts of employment.

The prophets and wisdom literature echo these exhortations: the gritty realism of Ecclesiastes, the encouragement of Proverbs to hard work and honesty, or warnings against exploiting workers (Isaiah 58; Amos 5). Human work is seen as 'fallen' because of human sinfulness, but also capable of redemption and transformation (Isaiah 65).

John Stott summarizes the biblical paradigm against which to judge the experience of work: for the fulfilment of the worker, to benefit the community, and to bring glory to God. While work in the Bible may seem far from modern employment contracts and task specialization, there is clear guidance applicable to any aspect of modern employment practice – not necessarily employment *policies* but employment *principles*:

- Creativity, dignity and purpose in work overcome the negative dimensions.
- Fair pay and treatment of workers.
- Protection of the weakest through minimum standards.
- Rest from work – the duty not to overwork.
- Efficiency less important than equity.
- Access to means of livelihood for all is not only a matter of rights or compassion, but of justice.

The current debate

How does our present experience of work in the UK measure up to this ideal? Three-quarters of the working-age population are in work – 29.4 million people. Of these, 25.4 million are employed by others (74 per cent full-time), with 3.8 million (13 per cent) self-employed. Part-time work has recently risen while full-time work falls, with growing numbers of part-time workers unable to find full-time work (over 10 per cent).[1] Over 2 million (6.5 per cent) are unemployed, a rise of 23 per cent or 369,000 people during 2008, and the highest for over ten years. The CBI and British Chambers of Commerce warn that the figure will exceed 3 million in 2010.[2] Unemployment in declining industrial and coastal communities is over twice the national average, three times higher among Afro-Caribbean than white males, and over four times more prevalent for disabled people.

Job opportunities are falling: vacancy levels plunged to 504,000 in January 2009. Meanwhile there were 259,000 redundancies in the final quarter of 2008, up 104,000 over the quarter. More people fear losing their job: in early 2009, 49 per cent of full-time workers were concerned about losing their jobs, up from 43 per cent in October.[3] Work-related stress, depression and anxiety waste 13 million working days a year, affecting half a million people, averaging 30 days per person. This costs employers around £3.7 billion; adding the public sector impact totals around £12 billion.[4]

Low pay persists, a quarter of all employees being on hourly earnings insufficient to keep them out of poverty unless they work long hours each week. The minimum wage provides a useful floor against exploitation, but campaigners in expensive areas such as London, Oxford and Cambridge argue for a higher 'living wage' above £7 per hour. After all, we rely heavily on many low-paid and vulnerable workers, especially in social care.

Those working long hours to overcome low wages make sacrifices in family life. Three-quarters of working families experience some weekend work, and in over half of these – 2.41 million families – at least one parent works regularly at weekends. Consequently children of weekend-working parents spend less time with their parents as there is no significant evidence of parents 'making up' for lost time on another day.[5] Half of all parents feel they don't spend enough time with their children. The 'Working Families' charity found that low-paid workers are least able to negotiate more family-friendly work hours.[6] The UK has among the longest working hours in Europe – despite the maximum 48-hour working week, because most can opt out 'voluntarily' and some jobs are exempt – finishing top of the table for weekend and night work.[7] The recession will increase pressure on workers to put in longer hours to protect their jobs.

The concept of work–life balance has grown over the past decade, with 'family-friendly' employment policies of unpaid parental leave and extended paid maternity/paternity leave introduced. Employees with a child under 16 or caring for a disabled child or relative now have the right to request flexible working. However, they must have been with their employer for over 26 weeks, and while employers must 'seriously consider' any application made, they may decline for 'good business reasons'. Encouragingly, around 85 per cent of requests are accepted by employers.

One key but neglected component of work–life balance is the shared day off. The Jubilee Centre's 'Keep Sunday Special' campaign inflicted the only Commons defeat on Mrs Thatcher, and thanks to their work Sunday remains distinctive with only six hours' trading by large stores. However, Sunday as a day of rest is better protected in countries like France which severely limit trade and see Sunday as a family day. EU legislation guarantees two days off every fortnight, not even one day a week – surely a minimum worth campaigning for. Nor is there a guaranteed weekend day off for working parents to spend time with their children – the Family Day Bill campaign seeks to change this.[8]

Other key battlegrounds are rights for part-time, agency and casual workers including EU migrants, improving child-care availability and funding, closing the gender pay gap, support for in-work training to increase skill levels, and the provision of in-work benefits to ensure that 'work pays'.

Policy to tackle unemployment is critical. Much debate centres on the degree of compulsion needed to encourage successful job-searching behaviour by unemployed people. Pressure is exerted through benefit levels, financial incentives and reduction of benefits for failing to seek work. Lone parents and incapacity benefit recipients are increasingly targeted with extra pressure to find jobs.

The government's record through its flagship 'New Deal for the Unemployed' has been relatively successful, with 1.85 million people helped into work, and long-term youth unemployment down from 23 per cent to 16 per cent since 1997. However, sustainable employment outcomes were proving difficult to achieve even before the recession began, and the policy is struggling to cope with reduced labour demand.[9] More active emergency measures being mooted include guaranteed jobs for graduates.

The Conservative Party has moved away from its reputation for 'on your bike' values where unemployment was 'a price worth paying' to reduce inflation. They now support the minimum wage and espouse making Britain the world's most family-friendly country. Along with the Liberal Democrats they support extending the right to request flexible working and longer parental leave which can be shared between parents.

How will each party respond to the recession: will employer or worker needs be prioritized? Will hard-won rights be threatened by re-establishing a strong market, or will the 'new' capitalism internalize social values and positive flexibility? What is a fair balance between the needs of employees and employers?

Christian response

Many of society's negative employment experiences relate to the very practices critiqued by the biblical narrative. For example, tolerance of low pay and long hours, unemployment persisting even in good times, and preventing asylum-seekers working while their claims are processed, which seems to contravene the gleaning principle of welcoming the 'alien' in need.

A biblically inspired employment basis for our society could embody the following priorities:

- Sufficient satisfying work for the greatest number possible.
- Work encouraged to serve individuals, families and communities, rather than people becoming enslaved to work.
- Absolute minimum unemployment, with meaningful activities for those not in jobs.
- Encouragement of a balance between partners in a family context to maximize the chances of healthy child-rearing.

Which policies are most likely to move us in that direction? Critical issues for rebalancing employment towards a biblical pattern to pose to our political and business leaders include:

- Sharing work more equally so 'hoarding' of hours and rewards becomes culturally unacceptable – *how will they advance this debate?*
- Encouraging greater family focus including shared time off – *will they fight for weekends and especially Sundays and flexible working?*
- Raising minimum wage and benefits levels as high as possible to ensure a dignified floor below which none should fall – *or do they believe this is bad for business?*
- Targeting unemployment assistance firmly and compassionately – *how far do they think compulsion is needed?*
- Raising skill levels (including basic literacy and numeracy) especially in poorer communities to break the low-skill/low wage trap – *how will they champion a sea change in aspirations?*
- Ensuring fair employment contracts to both sides – *do they believe that businesses or vulnerable employees should be prioritized?*

The Church, too, should strengthen its role in supporting people both in and out of work, and encourage social enterprises and charities seeking to create employment and training opportunities.

In conclusion, whatever is good and godly about work should ideally be experienced within what we now call paid employment. We should work with and lobby politicians and employers to promote work that – whether they acknowledge it or not – conforms more closely to God's pattern. Christians should be concerned about employment as a matter of justice and livelihood for all citizens, and how it helps or hinders the image of God in all human creativity. At its best, good work can set human spirits soaring; at its worst, bad work or no work can crush the soul. We should be pressing all our politicians to raise their sights.

Notes

1 Statistical data from LM Statistics, February 2009, ONS.
2 <http://news.bbc.co.uk/1/hi/business/7947766.stm> (accessed 24 March 2008).
3 MORI, 20 January 2009.
4 Health and Safety Executive data sheets.
5 M. Barnes, C. Bryson and R. Smith, *Working Atypical Hours: What Happens to Family Life?* (NatCen, 2006).
6 'Time, Health and the Family: What Working Parents Want' (Working Families, 2005).
7 'Weekend Workers: Part-time Parents', Relationships Foundation (<www.relationshipsfoundation.org>, accessed 1 June 2009).
8 More information on the proposed bill and associated campaign can be found at <www.keeptimeforchildren.org>.
9 In 2007, one in five people who found work through the 'New Deal' programme held a job lasting fewer than 13 weeks. A 2008 report by the OECD (*Jobs for Youth: United Kingdom*, Organisation for Economic Co-operation and Development, July 2008) noted that youth unemployment in the UK has risen from 11 per cent to 14 per cent since 2004, only 45 per cent of low-skilled youths find jobs after leaving school, and 13 per cent of 16- to 24-year-olds are not in education, employment or training.

Further engaging

Publications

David Jensen, *Responsive Labor: A Theology of Work* (Louisville, KY: Westminster John Knox Press, 2006)

John Stott and Roy McCloughry, *Issues Facing Christians Today* (4th edn), (Grand Rapids, MI: Zondervan, 2006), especially chapter 8, 'The World of Work'

Trades Union Congress employment research series, for example 'What Do Workers Want? An Agenda from the Workplace for the Workplace', September 2008

Work Foundation research papers, especially 'Hard Labour: Jobs, Unemployment and the Recession', Ian Brinkley, Naomi Clayton, David Coats, Will Hutton, Stephen Overell, November 2008

Christopher Wright, *Deuteronomy*, New International Biblical Commentary (Milton Keynes: Paternoster Press, 1996)

10

Housing

PETER LYNAS

Peter Lynas worked as a barrister before completing his MDiv at Regent College, Vancouver, where he studied the application of Old Testament ethics to the modern housing market. He is a researcher at the Relationships Foundation, Cambridge, and has written on a variety of policy areas.

Current debate

The British are obsessed with owning houses. There are people who simply 'do property' as a job, or at least did. We were spurred on by 'success stories' such as the Candy brothers who used a £6,000 loan from their grandmother to build up a property empire which owns 20 acres of prime real estate in central London and is valued in billions. Television schedules were filled with shows about buying, selling, renovating, building and decorating houses. It seemed that everyone wanted to be on the property ladder. The negative equity and high interest rates of the 1980s were forgotten: bricks and mortar were a 'sure thing'. The housing charity Shelter ran an advert suggesting that the average person was only four paycheques away from being homeless, but with house values rising by £100 a day, no one believed it. Then the bubble burst.

Changing times

The UK has seen a century of change in relation to housing. Between 1900 and 1998 the housing stock of Great Britain increased from about 7 million to 22 million permanent dwellings.[1] Owner occupation has grown from 10 per cent of homes in 1914 to a figure of 70 per cent in 1999, where it has levelled off.[2] Of the remaining homes, just over half are rented out by local authorities and housing associations, while the rest are rented out privately.

By 2020 the Office for National Statistics estimates that the population of the UK will have reached 67 million people. By the same date it is predicted that average household size will have dropped to 2.1. Based on these figures the UK will need 32 million houses – 7 million more than it currently has. That requires over half a million houses to be built each year, and means that the 3 million new homes promised by the government will be woefully inadequate.

Supply and demand

Demand has increased due to the drop in average household size caused by family breakdown, more people choosing to live alone, and people choosing to marry/cohabit later. It is also rising as the population lives longer, net immigration increases, and more people buy second homes. At the same time the growth in supply has fallen. House building peaked in 1968 when 413,700 new dwellings were built. In 2008 only 120,000 new homes were built and that number is expected to fall below 100,000 in 2009.[3]

The options are to increase supply by building more houses, raising questions in terms of the environment, transport, community and infrastructure, or to reduce demand by, for example, increasing average household size. Assuming that the population remains constant, an increase or decrease of 0.1 in average household size can affect housing need by 1 million houses. The reality is that both increased supply and reduced demand will need to be pursued.

There are not enough houses to continue living the way we live (in smaller and smaller units). Around 14 per cent of the population in England currently live alone compared with 6.5 per cent in 1971. Half of those living alone are of working age, while the other half are of pensionable age.[4] The rise in one-person households is expected to account for 72 per cent of annual household growth between 2003 and 2026. One-person householders consume 38 per cent more products, 42 per cent more packaging, 55 per cent more electricity, and 61 per cent more gas per person than an individual in a four-person household.[5]

Housing problems

The Times noted in 2006, 'Soaring house prices are thought to be a victimless phenomenon. In reality they represent a massive transfer of wealth to those who own property from those who do not. For the poor, home ownership is a receding prospect.'[6]

In 2007 almost 100,000 households were without a home.[7] Nearly 1.7 million households are currently on local authority housing waiting lists and almost 80,000 households are living in temporary accommodation.[8] Over half a million households in the UK are overcrowded, a figure which is likely to rise during the recession.[9] In England 8.1 million homes fail to meet the government's Decent Homes Standard.[10]

Given this, it is surprising to learn that there are 762,000 empty homes in England, nearly half of which are long-term empty.[11] These properties could house a million people. There are also 300,000 second homes across the UK and a further 193,000 second homes owned outside Great Britain.[12] If Britain's housing stock was fully utilized, no one would be without shelter. Houses are to be lived in, but have been reduced to purely economic significance (ignoring their social and, indeed, theological impact) and so are traded like any other commodity. Vacant property is a constant reminder of this commodification.

Biblical paradigm

The Old Testament repeatedly emphasizes the relationship between land and people. God gave Israel a land-holding system with the objective that every extended family should have an interest in a piece of land in perpetuity. In this way the future of individuals, families and the nation as a whole was to be secured. It is all the more ironic that this sense of place is the primary concern of a God who refused a house and sojourned with his people (2 Samuel 7.5–6), and of the crucified One who had nowhere to lay his head (Luke 9.58).

God and the land

Chris Wright has commented, 'Christianity has always wanted to talk about Yahweh and neglect land.'[13] The biblical text does not allow such neglect: the two are always in relationship, from the moment of creation. The promise of land is central to the covenant with Abraham; the Exodus begins a journey to fulfil that covenant promise. Israel's wilderness wanderings is a time of landlessness because of disobedience; this was not what God intended. Sinai explained the relationship between God, his people and the land. Instructions were given in anticipation of life in the land. Joshua narrates the conquest and division of the land, and Judges tells of the struggle to survive. Under David the full extent of the land is realized, but the monarchy also abuses this same land. The prophets protest the injustices perpetrated on the land and the Exile brings separation from the land as part of God's judgement. Isaiah blames those who 'add house to house, field to field' (Isaiah 5.8). Amos condemns those who trample on the poor while building stone mansions (Amos 5.11). Micah rails on the evildoers who 'defraud a man of his home, a fellow-man of his inheritance' (Micah 2.2). Return from Exile begins restoration of a sort, to both God and the land, but something more is clearly anticipated.[14]

Divine ownership

The basic biblical position is that God, the divine owner, gives a stake in the land/property to (Israelite) family units. God's ownership is clear and unambiguous. Leviticus 25.23 states, 'The land must not be sold permanently, because the land is mine and you are but aliens and my tenants.' The land is described as 'nahal', an inheritance. The Israelites inherited it from their ancestors and ultimately God, and held it on behalf of, and for the benefit of, their household.

Inherent in the Hebrew verb 'yarash', 'to possess', is the notion of 'to dispossess'. The Israelites were very aware that their interest in the land was at the expense of someone else. Jubilee reminded them that even land which they acquired was not theirs, but had to be returned.[15] The Sabbath year reminded them that God was the ultimate owner. Given the role of land for identity and economic viability, it could only be traded out of necessity (Leviticus 25). The moving of a boundary stone was such a serious offence because it dispossessed their neighbour and God (Deuteronomy 27.17). Boundaries were to be firm and yet porous. The poor were to be allowed onto the land to follow the harvesters and collect the gleanings (Leviticus 19.9–10, 23.22; Deuteronomy 24.19–22), and there was the right to satisfy one's hunger from a neighbour's vineyard or cornfield (Deuteronomy 23.24–25). On the Sabbath year, the poor and wild animals were to be allowed to feed off the land. Modern boundaries are much less porous. We are extremely reluctant to allow anyone onto our 'private' property, forgetting God's ultimate ownership, and that, for us to possess a house or piece of land, someone else is dispossessed.

New Israel

The New Testament picture of God as divine owner and giver remains the same. Our stake or interest is talked of in the same way; that is, as an inheritance. However, the land has changed radically. No longer will God's people inherit a specific land; rather the land has been 'Christified' and we are heirs to his kingdom (Matthew 5.3, 5, 10; Romans 4.13). A part of the socio-economic dimension of the land feeds through into corporate sharing and practical responsibility. The promise is no longer to the Israelites as a nation, but to the new Israel, all Christians. The strong family relation to land is now found in *koinonia* – fellowship.

There will be a new heaven and a new earth in which God will dwell among his people (Isaiah 65.17; 2 Peter 3.13; Revelation 21.1–3). In Isaiah's portrayal we will build houses and live in them, we will plant vineyards and eat their fruit, and will long enjoy the fruits of our work (Isaiah 65.21–22). He does not speak of disembodied spirits, but of worshipful work and creative activity. And Christ the King has come to inaugurate his kingdom, which is breaking into our world. It is 'now and not yet'. It is a future hope which impacts the present reality. 'Thus an eschatological interpretation of any Old Testament theme, such as land in this case, rebounds back into the present world with an ethical thrust.'[16]

Christian response

The biblical ideal was for land to be shared out among tribes and families, and then to be passed between generations. Land and family are inextricably linked: to destroy one is to destroy the other. In recent years Western culture has moved from thinking in large family units to smaller, nuclear family units. We have now reached the stage where life rotates around the individual. Our society suggests that an individual should be a land-owning, economically viable unit, a function that used to be fulfilled by the family unit as a whole. Our expectations of the individual are untenable. These unrealistic expectations cause more family breakdown and lead to individual despair.

Moving quickly to policy can be problematic. An example of this can be seen in relation to inheritance laws. Changing inheritance laws to make it easier for land to stay within families would seem an obvious modern application of the Jubilee laws. However, a simple law to this effect would only solidify current inequality. Changes would first be needed to arrive at a more equitable distribution, before considering making property transfer more difficult.

Ron Sider also reminds us that land had a wider meaning in the Old Testament. He argues that God wants every family to have the basic capital – land, money, knowledge – to earn their own way and be dignified, participating members of society.[17] Similarly, Brian Griffiths comments,

> As a result of industrialisation land has been replaced by capital as the most important means of production . . . In my judgment therefore the equivalent of this principle (that each family should have a permanent stake in economic life) today is the right of each family to home ownership, the need for more diffused and direct ownership of equity capital and the opportunity not just for a formal education but for retraining and post-experience training in later life.[18]

Policy

The comments above show the necessity of integrating the chapters in this book, but nonetheless we must explore a few housing policy ideas.

Housing supply

The first step is to fully utilize current housing provision. Local authorities can use Empty Dwelling Management Orders to take over private residential properties that have been vacant for more than six months and rent them out. Members of the public can also use a Public Request Ordering Disposal to force action with respect to the 100,000 empty homes owned by council housing associations and government departments. More houses must still be built, but we should create environmentally friendly, aesthetically pleasing mixed communities with buildings that help humans to live into the fullness of their humanity. New stock must include more family-sized units in contrast to the recent trend of building small apartments. There are also serious debates to be had about building on the green belt and areas such as floodplains. In general, these decisions are better made on a local level where there can be better accountability.

Social housing

The lack of social housing and the standard available are serious concerns. Overcrowding is a major issue in the sector. Children in poor housing are suffering from ill health and they are nearly twice as likely to leave school without GCSEs.[19] As the shortage has worsened, homes that become available tend to be allocated to people with complex social, economic and health problems, increasing the risk of community breakdown. At the same time, steps must be taken to overhaul housing benefit and the dependency culture. Recipients are reluctant to seek and take jobs because the impact on their benefits can be severe, the losses can exceed any gains. While those in social housing need a level of security, they must be encouraged to work. Social Homebuy schemes, which promote shared ownership and shared equity among social tenants and key workers, should be expanded. This allows people to acquire an affordable stake in a property.

Taxation

The UK taxation regime is broadly favourable to home ownership. Consideration could be given to abolishing stamp duty for first-time buyers rather than on houses of a certain value. Increased taxation on empty dwellings and second homes would discourage wasted resources. Local taxation should take account of the number of people in a house, not simply its value, and discounts for singles should be abolished.

Other ideas

In Britain 750,000 homes are occupied by several generations, with the figure likely to soar to 1.75 million by 2038.[20] Multi-generational living is a positive trend bringing extended families together. Local authorities and social landlords should take the social and welfare needs of extended families into account and enable them to live near each other by prioritizing their co-location. Reducing stamp duty or council taxes and increasing housing benefit for those who relocate close to an elderly relative could be considered. Tax incentives could also be provided for buildings that provide common public space – gardens, sculptures, open atriums and the like.

The parties have set out many of their housing proposals. They are all inclined to build more housing and improve the social sector. However, there is disagreement as to how improvements can be made, and there are questions as to the commitment of each of the parties. Housing is a major source of inequality. It may also cause intergenerational bitterness as young people are unable to afford to buy. The conditions in which too many people live in the UK should trouble us and challenge our own lifestyles. We must persuade our politicians that everyone deserves not simply a house, but a home. The biblical text reminds us of the importance of an integrated and long-term approach – families were given a stake in the land to secure their livelihood, dignity and identity from generation to generation.

Notes

1   *A Century of Change*, found at <www.parliament.uk/commons/lib/research/rp99/rp99-111.pdf> (accessed 11 June 2009).
2   Ibid.
3   'Number of New Houses to Plummet', *The Observer*, 28 December 2008.
4   Guy Palmer, *Single Person Households*, JRF 2006, p. 2.
5   <http://money.guardian.co.uk/ethicalmoney/story/0,,1834973,00. html> (accessed 22 July 2008).
6   'Duncan Smith Pins Down Britain, the Unequal Nation', *The Times*, 17 December 2006.
7   Statutory Homelessness Statistics, Communities and Local Government 2008.
8   Housing Strategy Statistical Appendix Data 2007, Communities and Local Government, 2008. Annual Digest of CORE Data 2006/07. Available at <www.core.ac.uk>.

9   Survey of English Housing Preliminary Results 2006/07, Communities and Local Government, 2007.

10 English House Condition Survey 2006 Headline Report, CLG 2007.

11 <www.emptyhomes.com/whatwedo/campaign_agenda.html> (accessed 10 April 2009).

12 'Tax Rise Threat to Second Homes', *The Times*, 17 April 2006.

13 Christopher J. H. Wright, *Old Testament Ethics for the People of God* (Nottingham: InterVarsity Press, 2004), p. 49.

14 Christopher J. H. Wright, *God's People in God's Land* (Grand Rapids, MI: Eerdmans, 1990), p. 4.

15 Though an Israelite could sell or, more accurately, lease the land, the Jubilee laws prevented him from permanently depriving his sons of their inheritance. The story of the Prodigal Son is a reminder that to claim ownership of your inheritance is to treat your father as dead (Richard Rohrbaugh, 'A Dysfunctional Family and its Neighbours', in V. George Shillington (ed.), *Jesus and His Parables: Interpreting the Parables of Jesus Today* (Edinburgh: T&T Clark, 1997). The father could transfer the land to the son during his lifetime but would have been entitled to a life interest in the land until his death. By selling off the land, the son deprived his father of his life interest, acting as if his father was dead. By acting as though they owned the land outright, the Israelites were acting as if God, the Father from whom they inherited their land by adoption, was dead (Exodus 4.22 speaks of Israel as God's firstborn).

16 W. D. Davies, *The Gospel and the Land: Early Christian and Jewish Territorial Doctrine* (Berkley: University of California Press, 1974), p. 186.

17 Ronald J. Sider, *Rich Christians in an Age of Hunger* (Dallas: Word Publishing, 1997), p. 121. See chapters 8 and 11 for further discussion of these ideas.

18 Brian Griffiths, *Morality and the Marketplace* (London: Hodder and Stoughton, 1982), p. 94.

19 <http://england.shelter.org.uk/__data/assets/pdf_file/0004/114853/ Child_Poverty_and_Housing.pdf> (accessed 10 April 2009).

20 *The Times*, 11 April 2008.

Further engaging

Publications

Walter Brueggemann, *The Land* (Minneapolis: Fortress Press, 2002)

Brian Griffiths, *Morality and the Marketplace* (London: Hodder and Stoughton, 1982)

Brian Griffiths, *The Creation of Wealth: A Christian's Case for Capitalism* (Downers Grove: InterVarsity Press, 1984)

Donald A. Hay, *Economics Today: A Christian Critique* (Vancouver: Regent College Publishing, 2004)

Andrew Henley, 'Piling up Treasure on Earth: The Crazy Ethics of the Housing Market', *Ace Journal*, No. 28, 2000

Michael Schluter and Roy Clements, *Family Roots or Mobility?* (Cambridge: Jubilee Centre Publications, 1986)

Michael Schluter and Roy Clements, *Reactivating the Extended Family: From Biblical Norms to Public Policy in Britain* (Cambridge: Jubilee Centre Publications Ltd, 1986)

Paul Williams, 'The "Homelessness" of Modern Britain', *Engage* (Jubilee Centre Publications, March 2004)

Christopher H. J. Wright, *God's People in God's Land* (Grand Rapids: Eerdmans, 1990)

Christopher H. J. Wright, *Old Testament Ethics for the People of God* (Downers Grove: InterVarsity Press, 2004)

11

Time for the Conservatives?

ALISTAIR BURT MP

I have always been wary of advising Christians how to vote, based on Christian values. There are believers in all our major parties, influencing our respective policies, and I agree with John Gummer who once wrote that we must distinguish between religious truth and political views, otherwise 'we shall claim for our mundane partialities a divine authority which ought not to dignify them'. But, with that caveat, perhaps I can help readers to feel at ease with a modern Conservative Party.

Change is in the political air. From time to time this country heads for a landmark general election, such as 1979 or 1997, which results not only in a change of government but in a national change of mood. The architecture for such change is often similar: length of time of a government in office, a crisis of some variety – economic or social, a recovery of confidence in a former party of government which has revived itself, or perhaps a clear contrast of personal leadership where public opinion moves decisively in favour of the new rather than the old.

I think all of these factors are now in place, and that David Cameron and my colleagues will make a strong bid for the support of the public at a crucial time in the country's economic and social history.

There is no doubt that the Conservative Party has been renewed through David Cameron's leadership, demonstrated in the direction which he has given, firmly rooted in the needs and concerns of the society we see around us. Care for the poor, the underprivileged and the downtrodden has characterized the Christian response since Jesus' parable of the Good Samaritan, and is at the heart of his teaching. At home, we have worked very closely with the Centre for Social Justice, led by Iain Duncan Smith MP, in its analysis of where parts of contemporary society have broken down. We have examined poverty, family breakdown, addiction, the care system, crime, prison, punishment and rehabilitation, looking not solely at the problems but at the solutions available through innovative work involving statutory agencies and increasingly the independent, faith and voluntary sectors. We are finding hope in the work going on in some of our poorest communities, but that work is often stifled by bureaucracy and a mindset which puts process before outcome. We are determined to change that, just as we are determined to make good our conviction that there is such a thing as society; it is just not the same as the state, which our opponents too often confuse. Mending those parts of our society which are broken is a priority, and is where we expect to work hand in hand with many Church agencies.

Increasingly we recognize that we live on a smaller globe, where we answer the call of 'Who is my neighbour?' by recognizing those half a world away as those to whom we have mutual obligations. Our international development commitment has been demonstrated physically through a remarkable initiative of David Cameron, making available the opportunity for Conservatives to volunteer in Rwanda over a period of three successive years. This has strengthened our commitment to achieving Millennium goals through NGOs and aid agencies, and reaffirmed our belief that only a combination of aid and trade (and we must see the Doha round completed, not stalled) will close the unjust gap in world wealth.

I have long believed that the Conservative approach to choice has a more than acceptable Christian basis. There was once a vogue to confuse absolute equality in all things with universal state provision as some exemplar of the 'New Jerusalem', until the sweeping away of Communist Europe exposed the reality and cruelty of such thinking. God allows us freedom of choice, and prizes the diversity of men and women. That there should be deemed just one way to provide essential services, from housing and health to education, seems odd, yet our opponents still seem reluctant to reward the citizen with real choice in public services, a sensible way of improvement.

Accordingly our proposals for greater parental choice in education, to create and run new schools, and to free professionals in health, the police, local government and other services from the absurd target and quota culture dictated from Whitehall should run with the grain of Christian belief.

It is perhaps in the realm of stewardship (Luke 16, 18) that we see two distinct Conservative challenges. We have moved the government on climate change and the marine environment, asking for testing goals on energy and alternative sources of power as we confront the enormity of our planet's future.

But it is on economic stewardship that we would most take the government to task. On Labour's watch this past 12 years we have seen the finest economy handed to an incoming government since the First World War simply dismantled. The failure to use the good times soundly, and to believe that 'boom and bust' could be ended on a mere say-so, meant that we were ill-prepared for the financial storms which have hit us, and the personal tragedies of unemployment as it soars. Our debt burden means that over a two-year period we will be borrowing more than governments over 300 years put together!

Enough. What we offer will be a responsible fiscal policy bolstered by independent oversight, a responsible financial policy underpinned by a renewed role for the Bank of England, and a responsible attitude to economic development that fosters more balanced economic growth.

In short, it is time for profound change. The present economic and environmental crisis is a clear call that we have not lived as we should have done, that we have taken God's world for granted, and squandered the 'talents' given to us. It will need a vast national effort to recover; which politicians, from our own acceptance of fault and responsibility, have a duty to lead. I believe David Cameron and my colleagues have the ideas, energy and policies to take on this burden, and the sense of service needed for national restoration.

12

Why Vote Liberal Democrat?

TIM FARRON MP

A huge problem in recent decades is that biblically inspired Christian concern for fairness and justice, compassion for those who are exploited and righteous anger at those acts of exploitation, have become, for some, a convenient excuse not to talk about those more awkward elements of Christian doctrine – issues such as personal morality and, fundamentally, the doctrine of man's sinfulness and of men and women being the rightful objects of the wrath of a righteous and holy God, and humankind's need therefore for salvation and the wonderful provision of that salvation through Jesus Christ.

To compound this, we have seen the opposite reaction, most notably among the 'Christian Right' in America, which has been to dismiss Christian concern for social justice as a woolly distraction from the need to preach the gospel and to stand up and be counted on personal morality issues. Both of these approaches are deviations from the truth.

The book of Amos reminds us that God's judgement of human sin is comprehensive, not selective. It is a standing rebuke to any of us who have sunk into accepting that it is apparently incongruous to be passionate both about correcting economic inequalities and social injustice, and about keeping God's laws on personal morality and preaching his word truthfully.

I am a Liberal and, like my Christian brothers and sisters in the other two parties, I am in a minority as a Christian in my party. We will sometimes be objects of ridicule or suspicion, but the great thing about being among Liberals is that you can rely upon them to defend your rights. As Christianity is sadly a minority faith, we must have legislators who instinctively favour free speech and the freedom of Christians to believe what we believe without fear of persecution. Some of what we believe with regard to sin, judgement and salvation is not exactly fashionable. From the non-conformist Christians of the nineteenth century, to the non-white immigrants, to the UK in post-war years, Liberals have championed the oppressed and been the defenders of unfashionable causes. Human freedom – including the freedom of individuals to choose and express their faith – is indivisible.

Edmund Burke said that 'all the laws against the Godless have not saved one single soul'. We cannot legislate to make people who are not Christians behave as if they were. God gives us free will, and as a Liberal I believe strongly that we have to allow all citizens to exercise that will – even if it offends our Christian sensibilities – so long as that behaviour is self-regarding and does not objectively harm others. As a Liberal Democrat I am appalled about our becoming a nanny-state. We were the only party that consistently opposed ID cards and fought against the growth in surveillance. We side with those unpopular minorities who demand to have their voices heard – we champion free speech and will not tolerate utilitarian attempts to override traditional British liberties.

Of course, you are not free if you are enslaved by poverty. Liberal Democrats understand that real freedom must be underpinned by fairness in our economy and by equality of opportunity in education. It is an outrage that it is still the case that the best way of guessing how a child will fare in life is to look at the income bracket of his or her parents. We must not tolerate this.

As a Christian, I want to support a party that is genuine in its passion for social justice – with apologies to my brothers and sisters in the other parties, you'd have to stretch credulity quite a bit to believe that social justice is what motivates a Conservative party that essentially exists to defend the powerful and the comfortable. Labour's record over twelve years, having overseen a widening of the gap between the rich and the poor and having increasingly supported authoritarian policies, means that they have effectively surrendered any claim to be the party of social justice or of progressive politics.

Liberal Democrats stand alone for a vision of a society where we seek to ensure a fairer distribution of our nation's wealth – and in fighting against unfair markets to ensure that there is a fairer distribution of wealth and opportunity between the nations too.

Secularists want us to believe that there is no place for faith in public life – that it should be airbrushed out of education and our daily discourse as at best an anachronism or more likely a pernicious threat to a free-thinking society. Secularism is not neutral; in fact, there is no neutrality. Everybody believes in something; everybody has a value system – they might not give it a name, but that makes no difference. We are all believers of one kind or another.

I believe in Jesus Christ as my personal Lord and Saviour. I also believe that while I am here, I need to represent him and to do with all my might that which I put my hand to. I note that all political decisions are based on values of one kind or another. The decisions that have directed our economy for the past 25 years, for example, have been based on a very particular set of values: principally greed and materialism.

The economic crisis we are experiencing now is a direct consequence of those values. Sadly, it was all very predictable. Margaret Thatcher and Ronald Reagan's economic experiment of the 1980s has failed in spectacular fashion. In fact, if we are to blame Gordon Brown for this recession – and I'm afraid that we must – then his most towering failure has been simply to adopt Conservative economics since 1997. Why should either of the parties who egged on this culture of greed, and allowed our entire system to be based upon it, be rewarded with power? The Liberal Democrats stand alone as the only party which predicted the recession, which warned against the economics of greed, and which has a practical plan to ensure that we avoid the inexcusable human misery caused by the recessions of the 1980s and 1990s.

Humbly, I would suggest that Christians should support the Liberal Democrats – not unquestioningly of course, but as a statement of our rejection of the shallow and amoral values that have led to the avoidable suffering that this recession has visited upon us; and as a statement of hope that genuine change is possible and that Britain can commit to a new understanding of 'community' where a fair deal for all, justice and commonsense economics can be embraced.

13

Why Vote Labour?

SHARON HODGSON MP

Party politics is often touted as facing something of a decline as we move into the twenty-first century. The strong success of single-issue campaigners who have led the way towards change on seminal global issues such as how best to combat climate change and bolster international development has seen the tribalism of traditional adversarial politics take a blow.

That is why I leapt at this opportunity to put forward the case for the Labour Party. Many of you will be familiar with the concept of the broad Church, and our party operates just like that. There is broad agreement on most issues but impassioned differences of opinion on others.

It is the case, though, that there are fundamental differences between the parties.

When asked to describe why I became a member of the Labour Party I could give many reasons, but none would be so succinct as simply to say, 'because I believe in fairness and social justice'. As former Labour Prime Minister Harold Wilson once said, 'The Labour Party is a moral crusade or it is nothing.'

Of course the Labour Party does not have a monopoly on morality but it undoubtedly has the strongest track record when it comes to delivering progressive social change.

In his chapter on the economy in this book, Paul Williams is right to say that we must view the current economic situation as one of opportunity, not just restraint. There are two types of economy in many people's lives: the invisible economy of national and global markets, and the very visible economy of household incomings and outgoings.

The events of the past year have shown how much one can

affect the other. We can't allow the culture of profligacy and recklessness to re-emerge in our financial institutions.

The G20 meeting chaired by Gordon Brown was a historic first where the countries of the world came together in recognition of their shared interests and the shared interests of their people. The regulations announced as part of the summit reflect Labour's belief that markets should be fair as well as free.

Paul also highlights our tendency to live for the weekend and view work simply as a means to make money. If we are to work towards a society where work is about more than the subsequent payslip, we need a strong and effective voice to represent those workers who feel undervalued, poorly treated or stifled in their creativity and potential. The trade union movement is an integral part of the wider Labour movement, and no one plays better the role of 'speaking up for those who cannot speak for themselves'.

Jonathan Burnside's chapter on criminal justice raises a series of interesting points. Much is made of the collapse of community values across the country. I know that in my constituency there remains a strong sense of community and the neighbours talk regularly, but we still face problems with anti-social behaviour and under-age drinking. It might sound a touch clichéd but I am sure we can all agree that delivering justice is about the proverbial carrot and stick. 'Labour favours too much of the carrot,' say the Conservatives, while Labour cries, 'The Conservatives are far too fond of the stick.' My own view is one which rides on the fundamental premise that no one is beyond redemption. We must strive to put in place a system which punishes but also protects.

Jonathan is quite right to say that effective justice will 'bring down the oppressor but liberate the oppressed'. Politicians are often criticized for their soundbites, but a memorable one for me was Tony Blair's promise to be 'tough on crime and tough on the causes of crime'. A key facet of any successful crime policy is the need to ensure that justice is seen to be done. Labour's introduction of Community Payback schemes whereby local communities choose the work undertaken by criminals on community service should help to strengthen that link.

Benedict Rogers' chapter neatly wraps up the major challenges currently facing the world. There is more than enough happening to which our eyes should be drawn. There remains large-scale oppression and withholding of human rights in authoritarian and dictatorial regimes across the globe. War crimes are still able to go unpunished, and genocide can still slip beneath the radar of the international community.

The election of a new American President gives us a cause for hope. So far Barack Obama has made clear his wish to see a reduction in the number of nuclear weapons and offered an olive branch to Islam after the bolshy rhetoric of the Bush regime. The values President Obama has shown strike a chord with progressive people across the world, and I hope he can continue to inspire a more positive outlook on global relations based on honesty and diplomacy.

The Labour Party's statement of values and aims reads:

> The Labour Party is a democratic socialist party. It believes that by the strength of our common endeavour we achieve more than we achieve alone, so as to create for each of us the means to realise our true potential and for all of us a community in which power, wealth and opportunity are in the hands of the many, not the few, where the rights we enjoy reflect the duties we owe, and where we live together, freely, in a spirit of solidarity, tolerance and respect.

No other party can claim to have these aims at its heart. The Labour Party is a party of equals and not elites. When considering the comments of colleagues during policy discussions, I am often reminded of 1 Timothy 5.21 which says, 'Be fair with everyone and don't have any favourites.'

Regardless of the policy context laid before you, it is worth remembering that the aim of the Labour Party is to make progress to a fairer society. That vision cannot be realized overnight; it is the quest of a movement.

Conclusion: How Do I Respond?

Hope, wrote Vaclav Havel, is

> a state of mind, not a state of the world. Either we have hope within us or we don't; it is a dimension of the soul, and it's not essentially dependent on some particular observation of the world or estimate of the situation.
>
> Hope is not prognostication. It is an orientation of the spirit, an orientation of the heart; it transcends the world that is immediately experienced, and is anchored somewhere beyond its horizons . . .
>
> Hope, in this deep and powerful sense, is not the same as joy that things are going well, or willingness to invest in enterprises that are obviously heading for early success, but, rather, an ability to work for something because it is good, not just because it stands a chance to succeed. The more unpropitious the situation in which we demonstrate hope, the deeper that hope is.
>
> Hope is definitely not the same thing as optimism. It is not the conviction that something will turn out well, but the certainty that something makes sense, regardless of how it turns out.
>
> In short, I think the deepest and most important form of hope, the only one that can keep us above water and urge us to good works, and the only true source of the breathtaking dimension of the human spirit and its efforts, is something we get, as it

were, from 'elsewhere'. It is also this hope, above all, which gives us the strength to live and continually to try new things, even in conditions that seem as hopeless as ours do, here and now.[1]

Votewise Now! seeks to assist readers to regain this sense of hope spoken of by Vaclav Havel. This biblical understanding of hope should inspire all of us to take our citizenship responsibilities more seriously, to seek wisdom and wise action in our homes, workplaces, churches, neighbourhoods and political parties. Such hopeful engagement is based on the fact that God desires all of his creation to have the ability to work and rest, to be liberated from the bondage of debt, to have the opportunity to live into their intended full humanity, to flourish in good relationships.

The general election is important – the outcome will shape our society for at least the next five years. The Christian community has an important role to play in the process. Here are some ideas:

- *Organize a husting*: many churches come together to organize hustings or debates involving the local candidates. If you are not aware of one in your area, get together with other church communities and arrange one – most candidates are happy to participate, regardless of their religious views.
- *Visit the party websites*: you can glean pretty quickly from the site what is important to the party and what message they are seeking to communicate.
- *Read the manifestos*: information is important; that's why we produced this book. As the election approaches, the parties will produce manifestos where you can find more detail on their policies.
- *Political discussions*: engage in and encourage others to debate the issues, regardless of how unqualified you may feel to do so.
- *Join a party/campaign*: some readers will be passionate about a particular party or candidate and will want to campaign for their election.

- *Stand as a candidate*: you are probably too late for this election, but should consider local elections and the next general election.
- *Vote!*

Most importantly, take time to dwell in the biblical text and allow it to instruct, challenge and inspire you to take its life-giving and hopeful vision forward into our society. This is the biblical mandate, to engage as 'salt' and 'light' at all times, and in all places. May you live, and vote, wisely.

Note

1   Vaclav Havel, *Disturbing the Peace*, trans. Paul Wilson (London: Faber & Faber, 1990), pp. 181–2.